Green Fiscal Policy and Firm Behaviour

This book is driven by the urgency of addressing the triple energy challenge—energy sustainability, security, and affordability. It explores a timely and policy-relevant research question, examining how effective green fiscal policies are in fostering the adoption of energy-efficient and environmentally sustainable technologies. *Green Fiscal Policy and Firm Behaviour: Towards Energy Efficiency* assesses whether such instruments are more effective when implemented in isolation or as part of a coordinated policy-mix, and investigates the right design, dosage, and sequencing of their deployment. The analysis centres on three principal fiscal instruments—environmental taxes, green investment subsidies, and green investment tax credits—and distinguishes between different types of green technologies, namely superior cleaner production technologies and inferior end-of-pipe solutions.

The book provides a comprehensive and empirically rigorous evaluation of green fiscal policies and their role in the green transition, framing them as a crucial corrective mechanism capable of bridging the gap between private and social returns to green innovation. It offers a comprehensive review of modern econometric methodologies employed in this growing field—including fixed-effects models, categorical treatment matching, difference-in-differences, complementarity, and sequential analyses—and contributes an original empirical study on the impact of fiscal rule changes on technology adoption outcomes. Lastly, it offers policy recommendations for the implementation of green fiscal policies.

This volume serves as a valuable resource for a broad readership, including graduate students, academic researchers, international organisations, and policy professionals—particularly those concerned with finance and the environment.

Kinga B. Tchórzewska is Assistant Professor in the Department of Finance at Kozminski University, Poland, and Research Associate at the Barcelona Institute of Economics. Her work focuses on energy economics, innovation, and public policy. She has published her work in leading journals and contributed to projects for the World Bank, the European Commission, and the OECD in the topics of green fiscal policy.

Routledge Focus on Economics and Finance

The fields of economics are constantly expanding and evolving. This growth presents challenges for readers trying to keep up with the latest important insights. Routledge Focus on Economics and Finance presents short books on the latest big topics, linking in with the most cutting-edge economics research.

Individually, each title in the series provides coverage of a key academic topic, whilst collectively the series forms a comprehensive collection across the whole spectrum of economics.

The Geoeconomics of Global Value Chains
Navigating Geopolitical Complexity and Industrial Policy Shifts
Katarzyna Mroczek-Dąbrowska

Dollar Dominance
Fundamentals, Nature and Present Structure
Junji Tokunaga

Resilient Global Supply Chains and Geopolitical Risk
Evidence from Central and Eastern Europe
Aleksandra Kania

Interest Rates and Asset Values
A Case Study in Closed Markets
Richard Thomas

Green Fiscal Policy and Firm Behaviour
Towards Energy Efficiency
Kinga B. Tchórzewska

For more information about this series, please visit: www.routledge.com/Routledge-Focus-on-Economics-and-Finance/book-series/RFEF

Green Fiscal Policy and Firm Behaviour

Towards Energy Efficiency

Kinga B. Tchórzewska

Routledge
Taylor & Francis Group
LONDON AND NEW YORK

First published 2026
by Routledge
4 Park Square, Milton Park, Abingdon, Oxon OX14 4RN

and by Routledge
605 Third Avenue, New York, NY 10158

Routledge is an imprint of the Taylor & Francis Group, an informa business

British Library Cataloguing-in-Publication Data
A catalogue record for this book is available from the British Library

Library of Congress Cataloging-in-Publication Data
Names: Tchórzewska, Kinga B. author
Title: Green fiscal policy and firm behaviour : towards energy efficiency / Kinga B. Tchórzewska.
Description: Abingdon, Oxon ; New York, NY : Routledge, 2026. | Series: Routledge focus on economics and finance | Includes bibliographical references and index.
Identifiers: LCCN 2026013114 (print) | LCCN 2026013115 (ebook) | ISBN 9781041195856 hardback | ISBN 9781041195870 paperback | ISBN 9781003712398 ebook
Subjects: LCSH: Fiscal policy--Environmental aspects | Business enterprises--Environmental aspects | Sustainable development
Classification: LCC HJ192.5 .T398 2026 (print) | LCC HJ192.5 (ebook) | DDC 339.5/2--dc23/eng/20260422
LC record available at https://lccn.loc.gov/2026013114
LC ebook record available at https://lccn.loc.gov/2026013115

ISBN: 978-1-041-19585-6 (hbk)
ISBN: 978-1-041-19587-0 (pbk)
ISBN: 978-1-003-71239-8 (ebk)

DOI: 10.4324/9781003712398

Typeset in Times New Roman
by KnowledgeWorks Global Ltd.

Contents

Figures and tables

Figures

Tables

1 Introduction

> Only sober societies can evaluate,
> others only worship or dishonor
>
> C.K. Norwid
> Letter to Jadwiga Łuszczewska, 19th July 1856

1.1 Research motivation

Green fiscal policy was born into a strange theatre. On one side, it is asked to carry the weight of extreme urgency, on the other it is judged inside the tight corridors of budgets, distributional conflict, industrial competitiveness, and electoral time. In that theatre, policies are rarely received with the one thing they need the most—sobriety. Carbon taxes are cast either as civilisational redemption or as technocratic oppression. Subsidies are either the engine of a new industrial age or a festival of rent-seeking. The public conversation, when it heats up, fired by ever-present social media, stops evaluating and begins adoring or condemning.

That is why this book begins with Norwid.

Cyprian Kamil Norwid—an outstanding 19th century Polish poet, playwright, essayist—wrote for much of his life from the margins of recognition. Exiled in Western Europe, he watched modernity assemble its machines, its markets, and its new languages of public life. Norwid's genius was not only lyrical, it was also diagnostic. He treated culture and politics as moral technologies, ways a society trains its attention and decides what counts as truth. His famous line about "sober societies" is a plea for clear-sighted rational judgement—for the civic capacity to distinguish evidence from intoxication and evaluation from allegiance.

Green fiscal policy demands precisely that capacity. It sits, in the end, at the centre of the three pressures that are often treated separately but in practice collide: energy sustainability, security, and affordability. As the global energy landscape evolves, energy efficiency is the quiet, structurally powerful

DOI: 10.4324/9781003712398-1

solution that speaks to all three pressures at once and can reconcile these objectives at scale. Yet, diffusion of energy-efficient technologies is not automatic. Cleaner process integrated production technologies often involve substantial fixed costs, uncertain payoffs, and organisational disruption. Firms hesitate not only because they doubt the technologies, but because the transition requires capital, skills, downtime, and coordination. As Rennings (2000) emphasised, the widespread diffusion of environmentally beneficial technologies is hindered by substantial fixed costs and uncertainty. This underscores the central role of green fiscal policies in facilitating both the development and deployment of such innovations.

This book takes sobriety in a deliberately technical sense—as a commitment to causal evaluation. The aim is not merely to assess whether policies appear to affect green technology adoption, but to examine *how we know*—and how fragile/strong that knowledge can be. Each methodology can present us in the end with a different angle, answering different research questions, and leaving different unanswered doubts. Thus, the question is not whether green fiscal policy sounds righteous or risky, but how, through which mechanisms and under which constraints, in what doses, in what sequence, it changes the pace and direction of green technology adoption—thus addressing the energy efficiency challenge.

1.2 Objectives

This section sets out the objectives and guiding research questions of the book. The objective is twofold. Substantively, its core aim is to explain how green fiscal policy instruments shape firm behaviour. The focus of this book is placed on industrial firms because they are major energy users and significant sources of pollution, making them an informative setting for evaluating how green fiscal policy affects both resource efficiency and pollution outcomes; thus contributing to elimination of the energy trilemma.

More precisely in Chapter 4, it tries to answer following four research questions. (1) Which green fiscal policy instruments most effectively incentivise the adoption of green technologies? Which type? (2) Does the proportional increase in green fiscal policy instrument drive higher levels of adoption of energy-efficient technologies? (3) What minimum policy "dose" is required to trigger measurable uptake of energy-efficient technologies? And (4) Can modifications of existing policy instruments be successful at skewing firms' investment into energy-efficient technologies? As we can see, the central theme is heterogeneity across technology types. The chapters ask, for example, whether stronger proportional tax credits shift investment towards cleaner-production (CP) and energy-efficient technologies, or whether they predominantly support inferior end-of-pipe (EP) abatement, and whether fiscal instruments can be redesigned to target high-impact efficiency upgrades while discouraging investments with weaker environmental returns.

The analysis then expands from single instruments to policy-mixes in Chapter 5. To that aim, it focuses on following three research questions. (1) Are green fiscal policy instrument complements or substitutes? (2) What are the complementary doses of green fiscal policy-mixes that increase adoption of energy-efficient technologies? And (3) Does the sequencing of green fiscal policy instruments over time matter for their effectiveness?

Finally, Chapter 6 formalises hypotheses around policy withdrawal, using as the example the phase-out of Spain's Environmental Investment (EI) tax credit to test whether removing the credit reduces investment in CP technologies, leaves EP technologies largely unaffected, and may generate an indirect, temporary increase in environmental Research and Development (R&D) as firms adjust. It also asks how does this phase-out affects firms under different policy-mixes and firm characteristics. The hypotheses are built in Chapter 6.

Methodologically, however, this monograph has a second objective that is equally important. Its goal is to assess not only what the empirical evidence concludes, but how those conclusions are produced. It therefore evaluates the identification strategies and empirical designs used across the book—what each method can credibly recover, which assumptions do the heavy lifting, and how sensitive policy inferences are to choices about timing, comparison groups, and treatment definition—so that the book's substantive claims about instrument design, intensity, mixes, and phase-outs are anchored in transparent methodological strengths and limits.

1.3 Scope

This book is about evaluation of green fiscal policy when the outcome of interest is green technology adoption. Its core concern is empirical—how researchers identify causal effects of taxes, subsidies, tax credits, and policy-mixes on eco-innovation—both CP and EP technologies—especially in the world where policies overlap, evolve, and are implemented under political and market shocks. Thus, this monograph adopts a mixed research design that combines (i) critical synthesis of the theoretical and empirical literature with (ii) quantitative, counterfactual policy evaluation grounded in modern causal inference. Methodologically, it proceeds in three linked steps. First, it develops an interpretive and diagnostic framework by reviewing key mechanisms and barriers to diffusion (e.g., fixed adoption costs, uncertainty, financial frictions, and externalities) and by assessing how alternative identification strategies map onto different causal questions. Second, it evaluates quasi-experimental and panel-econometric designs—such as fixed-effects models, difference-in-differences (DiDs) and their extensions (including triple differences), matching-based comparative designs, and related approaches for policy-mixes and timing—to recover policy-induced changes in green technology adoption under explicit assumptions and transparent counterfactuals. Third, it implements one of those designs to find novel empirical findings.

The scope is therefore selective by design. The book does not attempt to provide an encyclopaedic survey of all climate and energy policies nor does it serve as a general textbook on environmental economics. Instead, it focuses on the subset of public interventions that operate through fiscal channels—taxes, tax expenditures, and subsidies—and asks how these interventions shape firms' incentives to innovate and adopt green technologies, and how strong are the empirical findings we use. Where necessary, the discussion reaches beyond fiscal instruments to the broader policy environment—but the organising lens remains green fiscal policy and its evaluability.

Three substantive boundaries are important.

Firstly, the book emphasises uptake of green adoption and innovation at the firm level rather than economy-wide welfare accounting. Distributional concerns are important and reviewed in Chapter 3; however, this book does not offer a full general equilibrium welfare evaluation of climate and energy policies. Its ambition is narrower, but in a sense, more demanding, to clarify what the best available micro-empirical evidence can tell us about green innovation effects and just how confidently it can tell us.

Secondly, the book concentrates on empirical designs, measurement, and identification rather than on advocating for a single preferred instrument. It asks what different methods can identify, which types of research questions they answer, what threats to validity dominate in this domain (policy endogeneity, dynamic adjustment, mismeasurement of green behaviour, and heterogeneous effects), and how findings can be responsibly translated into policy recommendations. The aim is to equip the reader with a robust interpretive framework, to use it successfully in their own research and study evaluations.

Thirdly, the book treats policy as an architecture through time. Accordingly, it devotes particular attention to the evaluation of policy-mixes—static mixes and sequential mixes—and to the often-neglected empirical problem of policy phase-outs. Chapter 6 contributes novel empirical evidence on this dimension by analysing the phase-out of Spain's Environmental Investment (EI) tax credit and its effects on green technology adoption, using policy's withdrawal to illuminate firms' timing and heterogeneity—different responses across firms under different policy-mixes.

The intended outcome for the reader is practical and methodological. After finishing the book, the reader should be able to understand the main identification strategies used in the empirical literature, judge their credibility and limitations, and interpret empirical results in a way that supports policy learning—Norwid's "sobriety" in its modern, empirical form.

1.4 Structure

Having presented the research motivation, scope, and objectives, we can now turn our attention to the structure of the book, which follows a logical flow. The argument of the book unfolds in four movements: (1) general energy context motivating the research questions—the energy trilemma, (2) theoretical contributions on how policy instruments should work, (3) methodologies used to evaluate green fiscal policies, empirical results, and resulting policy implications before (4) turning to novel empirical evidence. I have intentionally woven the discussion of policy recommendations into the evaluation of methodologies, rather than isolating "implications" in a separate chapter, to emphasise a simple point. Every recommendation is only as credible as the empirical design and data that support it. Policy lessons do not emerge in a vacuum; they are conditioned by variables that a given dataset contains, the institutional setting in place, how a research question is framed, and which identification strategy is doing the causal work. Placing methods and implications side by side therefore forces a more sober interpretation—making clear where evidence is strong, where it is contingent, and where conclusions should be treated as suggestive rather than definitive.

Chapter 2 begins with the energy systems as the stage on which green fiscal policy must perform. It traces current trends in the energy markets through three pressures that are often treated separately but in practice collide: energy sustainability, security, and affordability, thus developing upon the research motivation. The chapter then develops a central proposition of the book's narrative logic—that energy efficiency is the quiet, structurally powerful solution that speaks to all three pressures at once. From there, it clarifies what is meant by eco-innovation, CP and EP technologies; and maps the principal barriers that keep such eco-innovations from diffusing—internal forces, external forces—especially financing frictions and existing externalities, building upon Rennings (2000).

Chapter 3 turns to the conceptual architecture that guides evaluation. Central to the discussion is the double externality theory (Rennings, 2000), which argues that diffusion of energy-efficient technologies is not automatic since green innovation requires public support at both the development and deployment stages. At the development stage, green innovation is often characterised by high uncertainty and significant knowledge spillovers, limiting firms' incentives to invest. At the deployment stage, the substantial fixed costs of adoption deter diffusion, also since the resulting environmental benefits are largely public goods, hence public policy is essential to address those market failures. It then reviews theoretical mechanisms through which individual green fiscal policies—carbon taxes, subsidies, and tax credits for green technology adoption are expected to affect green technology uptake. It then expands the lens to policy-mixes, because innovation rarely responds to a single instrument in isolation—in truth, we live in a world defined as "policy-mess" (Greco et al., 2022; OECD, 2025b). Firms respond to a multitude of packages, complements, and sequences at once. The chapter finishes with distributional concerns, within the causal framework, since incidence, liquidity, and political legitimacy shape not only who bears the costs, but also whether policies persist long enough to influence the investment horizons—hence, durability of public policies.

Chapters 4 and 5 are the methodological core. Chapter 4 evaluates the empirical strategies used to identify green fiscal policies and to translate the results into policy-relevant conclusions, for example, fixed-effects models, categorical treatment matching, instrumental variable (IV), DiD, and regression discontinuity design (RDD). The emphasis is on what evaluation really requires—right identification strategy, credible counterfactuals, careful measurements, and the ever-present right selection into treatment. Rather than treating methods as a menu, the chapter treats them as answers to existing challenges and institutional settings. It explains why particular identification designs are chosen, what issues they address, and what they leave unresolved. But also, which types of research questions are they capable of answering at all—the right dosage, what happens when a policy instrument is introduced, redesigned?

Chapter 5 extends this discipline to the methods used in the evaluation of policy-mixes—both static and sequential that evolve over time, including fixed-effects models with interaction terms, complementarity analyses, categorical treatment matching under double policy regime, difference-in-difference-in-difference methodology (DDD) and the sequential analysis, with the sequential methodology being the recent novelty (Lenihan et al., 2025b; Tchorzewska et al., 2025). It reviews how different methods intent to separate complementarity from mere correlation, how it handles interaction effects, and lastly it confronts the central difficulty of policy evaluation—that firms are not treated once—they are treated repeatedly. The chapter therefore examines empirical designs that can speak to timing, phase-ins, and phase-outs, while other instruments are present.

Chapter 6 moves the book's analysis from method and synthesis to novel empirical evidence. It presents new results on the phase-out of Spain's Environmental Investment (EI) tax credit and its consequences for green technology adoption, both cleaner production and end-of-pipe. Firms with different characteristics are investigated depending on their size and the number of green employees they hire. Most interestingly, firms under different policy-mixes are investigated. The chapter matters for several reasons. Firstly, it not only reveals how firms respond when a particular tax incentive is withdrawn, but it also tests policy design at the moment when support schemes are recalibrated, modified, or phased out–precisely when uncertainty, financing constraints, and strategic delay become most visible.

Chapter 7 concludes the monograph with a discussion of the final conclusions. It is not, however, the only place where the argument is consolidated. Each chapter ends with its own partial discussions of conclusions, so that the book builds cumulatively step by step towards the final synthesis.

1.5 Originality

The originality and value of the book rest on three pillars. First, it contributes novel empirical evidence from an independent work (Chapter 6). It draws on recently published empirical research—both the author's independent work and the author's contributions to collaborative team–based studies. The empirical chapters cover: the drivers of eco-innovation using fixed-effects model (Section 4.3.1), the proportional effect of the EI tax credit on uptake by using a combination of the IV approach with a DiD design (Section 4.3), the "dosage" of environmental taxation in stimulating green technology adoption estimated thanks to categorical treatment matching (Section 4.4.1), the impact of a modification to the EI tax credit while using the DiD method (Section 4.5.1), the effectiveness of policy-mixes at a given point in time by using fixed-effects model with interaction terms (Section 5.3.1), the minimum green fiscal policy intensity under policy-mixes while using categorical treatment matching (Section 5.3.3), sequential analyses of policy-mixes (Section 5.3.4), and finally, as was mentioned above, the effects of the EI tax-credit phase-out (Chapter 6). Sections 4.3, 4.5.1, and Chapter 6 present the author's sole-authored contributions. Chapter 6 also draws on original contributions by other authors. While these studies provide exemplary applications of modern empirical methods in environmental economics and the economics of innovation, their substantive scope extends beyond green fiscal policy and firm-level green technology adoption. This broader coverage reflects a persistent constraint in the empirical literature. Limited access to harmonised, policy-specific exposure measures and detailed firm-level technology data often prevents researchers from evaluating green fiscal instruments and adoption outcomes with precision. Accordingly, the book selectively incorporates these contributions where they illuminate transferable identification challenges and solutions relevant to the fiscal-policy–adoption nexus. The sections that rely on such evidence are IV approach to study an introduction of carbon pricing (Section 4.3.2), RDD to uncover the effects of R&D tax credits on general innovation (Section 4.4.2), DiD analysis to uncover the effect of an environmental tax with revenue recycling (Section 4.5.2), complementarity analysis of private R&D expenditures on eco-innovation (Section 5.3.2), and DiD with a policy-mix (Section 5.3.4).

Second, the book evaluates these contributions through the lens of methodological choice—making explicit how identification strategies, data structure, and empirical design shape what we can credibly claim about policy effectiveness. To my knowledge, this systematic linking of substantive findings of green fiscal policies to the toolbox of available methods has not been offered in one place before.

Third, the book speaks to a clear and still underserved research, economic and policy needs. As the OECD (Organisation for Economic Co-operation and Development) noted (OECD, 2025b), firm-level evidence on sequential policy-mixes and their productivity implications has been scarce if non-existent; although the literature on policy-mixes has expanded in recent years, major gaps remain—especially on sequencing and phase-outs. In the forthcoming years, the literature is likely to shift from evaluating single instruments to identifying the dynamic effects of policy packages and sequences (phase-outs and modifications), and towards better merging of firm-level data with measures of actual exposure to policy instruments from different sources, in order to distinguish complementarity from correlation and to credibly estimate not only energy-efficient adoption of technologies but also firm-level productivity effects.

1.6 Acknowledgements

This book would not have been possible without the support and goodwill of many people. I would like to thank the leadership of Kozminski University—Rector Prof. Grzegorz Mazurek, Vice-Rector for Research Prof. Paweł Korzyński, and the former Vice-Rector Prof. Robert Rządca—for their encouragement and institutional support upon my return to Poland after 12 years of studying and research abroad. I am especially grateful to my Head of the Department of Finance, Prof. Paweł Mielcarz, for sustained backing and for creating an excellent work environment.

I would like to express particular gratitude to Prof. Jose Garcia-Quevedo who has been a constant guide and source of academic care. I also thank my co-authors Prof. Pablo del Río, Prof. Ester Martínez-Ros, Prof. Marianna Marino, Prof. Pierpaolo Parrotta, Prof. Aneta Hryckiewicz, Prof. Domenico Buccella, Prof. Andrew Burke, Prof. Andre van Stel, Dr Yuvraj Pathak, Dr Shohei Yamamoto, and others—for the intellectual partnership that not only shaped several of the empirical chapters in this volume but also heavily influenced me as a researcher and inspired me to grow.

I am grateful to Prof. Jacek Tomkiewicz, Prof. Krzysztof Jackowicz, Prof. Oskar Kowalewski, Prof. Krzysztof Szczygielski, Prof. Adam Zaremba, Prof. Paweł Krzyworzeka, and Prof. Barbara Będowska-Sójka for their support over the past few years, while surfing the Polish waters for the first time, and to Dr Olga Rodak for inspiring me to write this book in the first place. I also acknowledge, with appreciation, the financial support provided by Poland's National Science Centre (NCN) and the Ministry of Science and Higher Education (MNiSW), through grants (OPUS 29, 2022/45/B/HS4/00154 as PI) and the scholarship for Outstanding Young Scholar after my return to Poland, which helped fund research activities related to parts of this monograph. As well as research awards including Kozminski Award for publishing in a Financial Times Top 50 Journal Ranking financed by Prof. Andrzej Koźmiński. I would also like to thank INE for access to data.

Finally, I would like to thank the administrative team at Kozminski University—Ms. Beata Chmura, Ms. Katarzyna Dąbek-Olender, Ms. Magdalena Klimaszewska, Mr. Andrzej Krzyżewski, Ms. Kinga Nekanda-Trepka, Ms. Marzena Ostopinko, and Ms. Anna Tybuś-Kamela—for their professionalism, kindness, and invaluable help over the past few years.

2 Energy trilemma and energy efficiency

2.1 Introduction

Contemporary energy and climate policies are no longer just about ensuring security of supply, but also about doing it cleanly, reliably, and affordably. This chapter takes the energy trilemma, sustainability, security, and affordability, as its starting point and aims to explain what role energy efficiency and eco-innovation can play in easing that three-way tension. Section 2.2 sketches the technological, market, and geopolitical shifts currently reshaping energy systems and presents them as challenges to the energy trilemma. Against this backdrop, Section 2.3 introduces energy efficiency as a first-best lever on the demand side and clarifies the notion of eco-innovation—distinguishing between cleaner-production (CP) from end-of-pipe (EP) solutions, and Section 2.4 reviews the barriers that prevent cost-effective efficiency measures from being adopted. Finally, Section 2.5 offers conclusions from the chapter.

2.2 Current energy landscape and challenges to energy trilemma

2.2.1 Energy trends

The energy story of the mid-2020s is one of acceleration and friction at once. On the acceleration side, renewables are scaling at record pace (Figure 2.1) and electricity is taking a larger share of final energy, thus quickly decarbonising the grid. The International Energy Agency (IEA) reports that renewables produced about 30% of global electricity in 2023 and are on track for around 46% by 2030, with solar and wind providing almost all the increase (IEA, 2024a). These trends are projected to increase, with annual renewable capacity additions forecast to rise from about 666 gigawatt (GW) in 2024 to nearly 935 GW by 2030 (IEA, 2024b).

At the same time, electricity demand is also rising, having reached 4.3% in 2024—a step-up from 2023—and is expected to grow at ~4% per year through 2027, driven both by increases in demand per person through electrification,

DOI: 10.4324/9781003712398-2

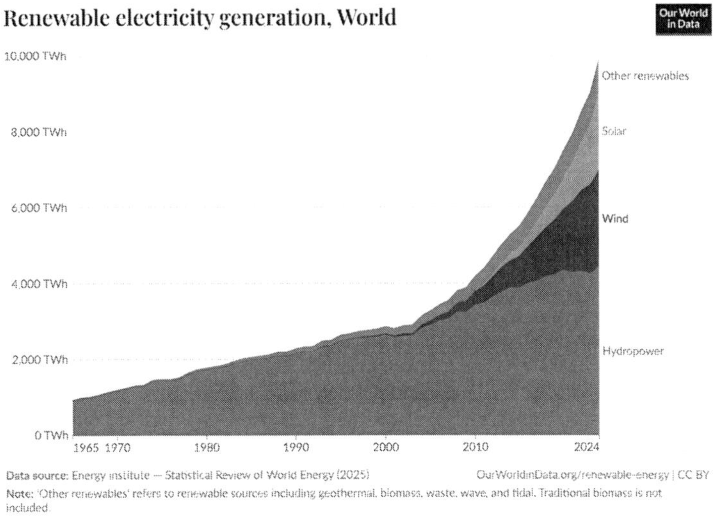

Figure 2.1 Renewable electricity generation across the globe

(*Source*: Our World in Data, 2025)

air conditioning, industrial activity, and the expansion of data centres (IEA, 2025a, 2025b); as well as increases in energy demand from population growth itself.

With regard to population growth, it adds a steady but steep background push to energy demand. Current demographic benchmarks put the world at about 8.2 billion people in 2025; with United Nations (UN)-based projections suggesting around 9.6 billion people by 2050—roughly a 17% rise in head-count, which (all else equal) would translate into a similar order increase in energy demand if per-capita use were constant (Suzuki & Pirlea, 2025).

But all else equal rarely holds, IEA emphasises that energy demand per capita is generally lower in emerging and developing countries; yet, these are precisely the places experiencing rapid urbanisation, expanding infrastructure, and progress on access. Meanwhile, recent demand dynamics underline how strongly per-capita factors shape electricity use. We can see it especially in developed economies, where population growth is relatively stable and therefore cannot explain large swings in demand. Against that backdrop, the outlook for electricity consumption by data centres, AI, and cryptocurrencies is particularly concerning, especially having the energy trilemma in mind. These loads are projected to rise from roughly ~460 terawatt-hour (TWh) in 2024 to >1,000 TWh by 2030 (IEA, 2025c; Noland et al., 2024), as shown in Figure 2.2. In the base scenario, demand should reach about 1,900 TWh per year by 2035—around 70% of the European Union's (EU's) current annual

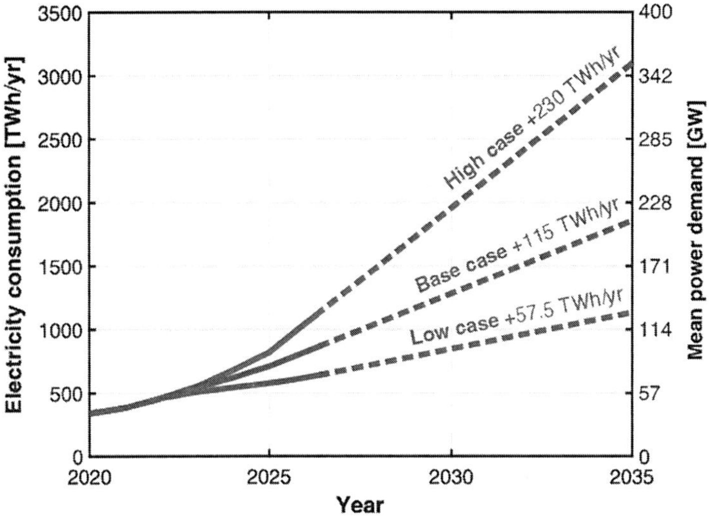

Figure 2.2 IEA's projected annual electricity consumption and mean power demand from data centres, artificial intelligence (AI), and cryptocurrencies until 2026, with linear extrapolations towards 2035 for high, base, and low cases

(*Source*: Nøland et al., 2024)

electricity generation—and scenarios above the base imply system-scale growth accumulating year after year. This is particularly concerning from the energy-efficiency perspective—each additional kilowatt-hour increases the need for clean generation, grid capacity, and system flexibility, and it can exacerbate congestion and reliability stresses in already constrained networks. From a system-planning perspective, lower demand growth is preferable because it translates into fewer new clean plants to build, fewer curtailment hours, and lower system emissions for the same level of energy service (IEA, 2024c).

2.2.2 *Challenges to energy sustainability, security, and affordability*

As we mentioned, the energy story of the mid-2020s is one of acceleration and friction at once. Frictions are increasingly visible as we integrate renewables more. First are the frictions impeding energy sustainability. The common challenge is the local resistance—the so-called *NIMBY*[1] dynamics. It can be slow permitting, turning even widely supported clean energy goals into contested, place-bound negotiations (Jarvis, 2024). It is true that compensation and greater local ownership can help in reducing this challenge; but higher energy efficiency shrinks this sitting problem directly. Each megawatt-hour avoided is one that does not need land, consent, and grid connection—reducing conflict pressure while lowering the amount of capital that must ultimately be recovered through bills.

A second constraint is the grid fit. Legacy grid systems were largely built around conventional plants that could be located near demand centres, requiring relatively limited new transmission. By contrast, wind and solar are often produced where resources are most abundant (offshore, deserts, and sparsely populated regions). These renewable-abundant zones are frequently poorly integrated with load centres, leading to transmission frictions. A recently published study of Gonzales et al. (2023) not only highlights this aspect but also presents it as an associated timing problem. The authors use solar panels' data from Atacama desert (Chile). When generation increased more quickly than the wires were constructed, local prices and curtailment signalled avoidable friction. Energy efficiency here is the companion policy to grid expansion. By reducing and reshaping load in congested nodes, it increases the usable share of renewables, frees scarce transfer capacity while lines are planned and permitted, and can defer to downsize network upgrades.

The third constraint to energy sustainability is intermittency and balancing. Because wind and solar output are variable (intermittent), scaling them up intensifies the need for flexibility—through storage, dispatchable backup, demand response, and stronger interconnections—yet, these enabling technologies and the supply chains behind them do not expand overnight (Petersen et al., 2024). In this sense, friction shows up most tangibly in networks and supply chains, which have also become central to energy security. The IEA estimates that at least 3,000 gigawatt (GW) of renewable power projects—around 1,500 GW at advanced stages—is stuck in grid connection queues worldwide (International Energy Agency, 2023). Having this in mind, the IEA argues that meeting climate targets now hinges on easing this infrastructure friction. Global annual grid investment needs to nearly double to over USD 600 billion by 2030, and the world must add or replace around 80 million km of power lines by 2040—roughly the scale of today's entire grid.

However, the frictions arise not only downstream in networks, but also upstream in supply chains that support energy security. As clean technologies scale, the demand for critical inputs rises quickly—IEA reports lithium demand rose by about 30% in 2023 (IEA, 2025d)—while refining and processing remained highly concentrated. This creates security risks across batteries, power electronics, and heat pumps. This is where efficiency and flexibility could reduce friction most directly. Shaving peaks and enabling demand response can free scarce grid capacity in the short run (often deferring the most urgent network upgrades), while lowering overall demand reduces exposure to imported fuels and shrinks the volume of hardware—and minerals—that the system must procure and finance.

With regard to another enduring energy security, we must also remember that the world's fossil reserves are concentrated far from where energy is most heavily consumed. Nearly half of proven oil reserves are in the Middle East (≈48%), with another ≈18% in Central and South America; for natural gas, the Middle East holds about 40% and Russia/former Soviet Union around 30%, while demand is concentrated in the OECD and large emerging economies such as China and India (Energy Institute, 2024). This mismatch makes import dependence—and exposure to price and geopolitical shocks—structural. Europe's experience since 2022 shows both a significant vulnerability and the adaptive capacity of our modern systems. The continent suffered an energy crisis due to energy price spikes, but the EU, in a relatively short period of time, managed also to diversify gas supply via liquefied natural gas (LNG) and alternative pipelines, expanded interconnection, compressed demand, and accelerated renewables through REPowerEU and related measures (European Commission, 2022). As we have mentioned, security is also increasingly a grid story. Congestion, connection queues, and balancing can all lead to scarcity locally even when generation is ample, and evidence from Chile shows that interconnection can quickly reduce costs, integrate renewables, and cut emissions (Gonzales et al., 2023). Finally, Tchorzewska et al. (2026a) show that elevated water temperatures can raise the risk of unplanned coal power plant outages by constraining cooling capacity. This is particularly concerning because similar thermodynamic bottlenecks may plausibly apply to nuclear plants as well, adding a further, climate-linked friction to energy security. The same mechanism also carries a sustainability cost. Unplanned coal outages are associated with higher local pollution burdens in densely populated regions, where marginal damages are likely to be especially large (Tchorzewska et al., 2026b). Taken together, these frictions sharpen a conclusion that demand reductions delivered through energy efficiency provide security benefits immediately, by easing stress on the system before new supply or networks can be built.

As electrification and new loads grow—through electrical vehicles (EVs) and data centres in particular—adequacy and flexibility become central. The IEA projects rising peak demand and much faster growth in short-term flexibility needs as intermittent renewables expand (IEA, 2024a). Data-centre electricity use is expected to roughly double by 2030 in the base case (IEA, 2025a, 2025b). Meanwhile, clean-tech supply chains remain concentrated (e.g., battery materials), adding a materials-security layer to the trilemma (IEA, 2025d). Across these domains, energy efficiency and flexible demand seem to be security instruments. They both shrink import exposure, relieve congested networks, reduce curtailment and balancing volumes, lower the storage and grid capacity needed, and reduce the hardware and minerals the system must procure—advancing sustainability and affordability at the same time. Hence, across fuels, networks, weather, supply chains, and new loads, energy efficiency translates into higher security. It reduces volumes of trade that must clear in volatile global markets (affordability), creates headroom on stressed national networks (security), and raises the emissions payoff of every clean kilowatt-hour delivered (sustainability).

Affordability remains the third, ever-present leg of the energy trilemma. The latest global Sustainable Development Goal 7 (SDG7) assessments show that energy access and affordability progress are uneven, with ~685 million people still lacking electricity access in 2022 (projected to 750 million) and ~2.1 billion relying on polluting fuels for cooking—exposures that translate into vulnerability to price swings for households and small and medium-sized enterprises (SMEs) worldwide (World Bank et al., 2024). Additionally, since the energy crises of 2022, due to energy price spikes and consequently the higher inflation rates in spite of temporary price shields, we can observe for the first time in years, increasing energy poverty even among the developed economies (European Commission, 2025). In 2023, the percentage of people reporting that they cannot keep their home adequately warm within the EU jumped to 10.6%. Thus, energy affordability touches the daily life—in payslips and invoices—in whether a single parent heats every room of the house. Efficiency upgrades to homes and appliances, thus become, anti-poverty policy as much as climate policy. Efficiency also addresses the costs that are not direct—those bills we do not see—the capital cost embedded in the system. Clean generation typically has low operating costs over its life, but financing needs are substantial—especially with higher interest rates since 2022. Thus, every unit of energy avoided means less investment required in generation, grids, production lowering both operating expenditure and the capital base that must be recovered from consumers.

2.2.3 *Energy-efficiency gap*

Meanwhile, the pace of global energy-efficiency improvement has weakened. Primary energy intensity fell by only about 1% in both 2023 and 2024—roughly half the average rate in 2010–2019, and far below what would be consistent with 2030 goals (IEA, 2024d). This deceleration matters because, under tight energy and grid conditions, each percentage point of demand avoided tends to deliver system benefits faster than most supply-side options can be planned, permitted, and built. It reduces fuel imports, relieves congestion, and lowers bills. In this respect, efficiency is the most immediate way to compress the energy trilemma—cutting emissions at once, strengthening resilience by reducing volumes flowing through stressed infrastructure, and containing costs by shrinking the CapEx (Capital Expenditure) and OpEx (Operating Expenditure) ultimately recovered from consumers.

Yet, these gains do not arise automatically, because the energy-efficiency gap persists. The term captures the recurrent finding that many investments that look cost-effective—sometimes even "negative-cost" on paper—are not adopted in practice, as private decisions diverge from the social optimum

(Jaffe & Stavins, 1994b). Part of the gap is structural due to market failures, for example, split incentives (e.g., landlord–tenant), imperfect information, financing constraints, or organisational frictions raise effective hurdle rates and delay action; part may reflect unobserved costs and heterogeneous preferences that standard calculations miss (Allcott & Greenstone, 2012; Gillingham & Palmer, 2014). Either way, when efficiency is systematically underdelivered, the system we must build becomes larger than necessary—more contested projects to site, more kilometres of wires to finance and permit, and more time operating near the margin. Energy efficiency makes clean supply both more governable and more valuable.

2.3 Eco-innovations

Having clarified why energy efficiency deserves centre stage, the chapter now moves from diagnosing trends and frictions to asking which technologies could be helpful in achieving energy efficiency. The focus is on eco-innovation, and in particular on CP technologies—process-integrated, preventive changes that reduce resource use and pollution *before* they occur; though EP technologies are also discussed (Frondel et al., 2007).

2.3.1 Defining eco-innovation, cleaner-production and end-of-pipe technologies

In line with the Eco-Innovation Lab's formulation, eco-innovation denotes new or significantly improved products, processes, organisational practices, or business models that reduce environmental burdens and resource use across their life cycle while creating economic value. In the following book, we are concerned with process eco-innovations, thus those that are relevant in the production process.

Process eco-innovations, on one hand, provide better performance for the firm, on the other hand require less energy, material, and produce less pollution per unit of service, which is why green innovation is shown to be social welfare enhancing (Buccella et al., 2024; Tchorzewska, 2020). This is clearly shown in Figure 2.3 presenting added value from eco-innovation. Those typically include—new investments, increases in productivity and technical capacity—hence, international competitiveness, accessing new and emerging markets, increasing profitability along the value chain, and staying ahead of standards and regulations.

Process eco-innovation is an umbrella concept, but the literature typically distinguishes between Cleaner Production (CP) and End-of-Pipe (EP). Firms often combine EP for short-run compliance with CP for longer-run efficiency gains once investment and organisational capacity allow. Cleaner production (CP)—also called process-integrated or preventive innovation—reduces pollution and resource use at source by changing inputs, processes, controls,

Figure 2.3 Added value from eco-innovation

(*Source*: UNEP, 2025)

or products; thus, it is often viewed as superior though radical, since they radically change the production process (Frondel et al., 2007; Horbach, 2008; Rennings, 2000). CP includes energy- and resource-efficiency upgrades—e.g., heat integration and recovery, process control, heat pumps, and electrification—plus management practices such as ISO 50001 (Bashmakov et al., 2022; IEA, 2025e; IOS, 2018; UNEP, 2007). We need to remember it is an umbrella term that can have many subcategories.

End-of-pipe (EP) (abatement) instead adds downstream equipment that captures or treats emissions after they are generated, serving mainly compliance and environmental protection goals rather than efficiency (Frondel et al., 2007). EP includes stack/vent/drain controls (e.g., flue gas desulfurization (FGD), selective catalytic reduction (SCR)/selective non-catalytic reduction (SNCR), and wastewater treatment) and generally treats symptoms without improving underlying productivity (IPCC, 2005; Metcalf et al., 2014; OECD, 2022). Thus, it is costly, but apart from reducing pollution, it does not affect the firm directly.

2.4 Challenges to energy efficiency

2.4.1 *A map of barriers*

The empirical literature typically maps the determinants of eco-innovation—its drivers and barriers—onto a distinction between internal and external factors (del Río et al., 2021; de Marchi, 2012; Horbach, 2019; Horbach et al., 2012). This distinction matters because the forces that make eco-innovation attractive (productivity gains, competitiveness, reputational benefits, and—often—higher long-run profitability) do not automatically translate into adoption. For many firms, especially SMEs, the problem is not a lack of incentives in principle but the presence of binding constraints. Eco-innovation is a rational option that remains out of reach because the organisation cannot absorb the upfront costs, the implementation risk, or the managerial complexity that the transition requires—which is especially problematic for smaller firms.

Within the set of internal barriers, the literature repeatedly returns to the firm's resource and capability base—its relevant competence and capabilities (RCCs) and the complementary assets that make technical change feasible (Horbach et al., 2012). This includes not only hard resources such as finance, physical capital, and production assets, but also soft and often scarcer ingredients, such as the technological know-how, data, and skills, organisational routines, and the ability to redesign processes without disrupting output quality or delivery schedules. Equally important are relational assets—customer relationships, supplier ties, and informal networks—that shape access to information and credible partners when experimenting with new technologies. Reputation enters here also as an economic variable, since it affects trust, the willingness of banks and investors to extend credit, and the perceived risk of financing projects whose returns depend on learning-by-doing. Finally, the literature highlights managerial commitment—especially top management's orientation towards environmental performance—as a catalytic factor that determines whether eco-innovation is treated as a peripheral compliance project or as a strategic investment worthy of attention, coordination, and capital (Bossle et al., 2016; Cai et al., 2018; del Río et al., 2021; Hojnik & Ruzzier, 2016; Horbach et al., 2012).

Across this literature, there is an agreement that external conditions often matter more than internal intentions. Even capable firms with motivated managers tend to move only as fast as their stakeholders and policy environment makes it rational and feasible to do so. Eco-innovation is a response to signals coming from outside the firm, for example, environmental authorities and the credibility of enforcement, the design of rules and standards, industry associations that diffuse norms and information, customers who reward (or ignore) greener products, and competitors whose moves reset what counts as best practice. In this sense, external factors shape not only the *profitability* of eco-innovation but also its *timing*. They determine whether the expected returns are secure enough to justify irreversible investments and whether laggards can continue to free-ride on weak oversight.

Regulation is central here because it structures both risk and opportunity. Well-designed environmental rules can create a predictable horizon in which firms invest in cleaner processes, while poorly designed or weakly enforced rules can encourage delay and incrementalism (e.g., through EP). Market-based instruments—such as environmental taxes, tax credits, subsidies, and grants—operate through the same channel, they change relative prices, compress payback periods, and reduce uncertainty around adoption, whereas their absence leaves firms facing the full upfront cost and learning risk of cleaner technologies (Peñasco et al., 2017; García-Quevedo et al., 2022). More subtly, policy-mixes and their stability matter, eco-innovation depends on planning cycles, financing windows, and supplier relationships, so frequent rule changes or short-lived support schemes can deter investment even when headline incentives look generous. In short, external factors work as the economy's "permission structure" for eco-innovation—setting the boundary conditions within which internal capabilities can actually be mobilised.

What is interesting, Porter and van der Linde (1995) argued that well-designed regulation can do more than impose costs—by pushing firms to rethink products and processes, it can induce green innovation that partially—or even fully—offsets compliance costs through higher productivity, lower material and energy use, and improved product quality. In its "weak form," the hypothesis predicts that stricter regulation increases environmental innovation, whereas in its "strong form," it suggests that the resulting innovation can raise competitiveness and sometimes even profitability—rather than erode it. In the last 30 years, there have been empirical studies proving that the properly designed green fiscal policies can achieve just that under certain conditions (Martin et al., 2014; Yamazaki, 2017).

2.4.2 *Finance as the binding constraint*

Across countries, financial constraints are the most frequently reported obstacle to eco-innovation (Ghisetti et al., 2017; Kiefer et al., 2019). High upfront costs, thin internal cash flow, and limited access to external funding slow or stall projects with otherwise attractive life-cycle economics (Souto & Rodriguez, 2015). Better financial health is consistently associated with higher eco-innovation propensity (del Río et al., 2015; Frondel et al., 2007). Managers who perceive tight finance are more likely to be laggards than leaders or fast followers (Triguero et al., 2013), and access to capital is positively correlated with eco-innovations across environmental domains and energy subsectors (Frey et al., 2013).

Because financial strength scales with firm size, SMEs and young firms face tighter constraints—financial, technological, and managerial—and often experience weaker stakeholder pressure to "go green" (Cainelli et al., 2015). The result is a robust size premium in adoption rates, in Spain (Cuerva et al., 2014; del Río et al., 2021; Jové-Llopis & Segarra-Blasco, 2018; Souto &

Rodriguez, 2015; Triguero et al., 2013) and elsewhere (Horbach, 2016). In other words, the firms with the highest aggregate savings potential (SMEs) often face the highest per-project frictions.

2.4.3 Beyond money—Externalities

As we will also see in Chapter 3, barriers to green technology adoption are not only a matter of internal capabilities and external policy or market conditions. There is an additional, more structural source of underinvestment that is closely entangled with finance—the double externality of eco-innovation that we will discuss in detail in Chapter 3 (Rennings, 2000). The core claim is that eco-innovation tends to be systematically underprovided because it produces two distinct spillovers that depress private returns: knowledge and environmental externalities.

2.5 Conclusions

This chapter has argued that energy efficiency is the organising principle of a credible energy transition. Read through the energy trilemma—sustainability, security, and affordability—the same conclusion repeats. A system that needs less energy to provide the same or better services is easier to decarbonise, easier to secure, and cheaper to run.

First, on current market trends, we saw a world of acceleration and friction. Renewables are scaling quickly and electrification is widening the share of end-uses that depend on electricity, yet networks and supply chains are straining. In that context, each avoided kilowatt-hour eases grid constraints, reduces curtailment, and lowers the clean capacity we must add. Energy efficiency therefore multiplies the impact of every euro invested in supply.

Second, on energy security, we showed that security has become as much a network and demand problem as a fuel problem. Shocks propagate through prices, grids, weather events, and geopolitics. Energy efficiency—especially peak shaving, flexible demand, and hardening of buildings and processes—acts as reliability. It trims import exposure, frees scarce transfer capacity, and reduces the need for emergency, high-carbon generation.

Third, on affordability, we traced how price spikes translate into inflation, tighter household budgets, and fiscal outlays. Temporary price shields help, but only structural demand reduction—via efficient buildings, appliances, processes, and well-designed demand response—decreases bills permanently. Energy efficiency also shrinks the capital bill the system must carry in generation and grids, moderating tariffs over time.

Fourth, we clarified what kind of innovation delivers those savings inside firms. Eco-innovations come in two families. Cleaner production (CP)—process-integrated, preventive change—reduces energy, materials, and emissions at source. End-of-pipe (EP)—add-on abatement—captures pollution after it is formed. Both are necessary, but if the aim is to use less energy for the same output, CP is the engine. It cuts operating costs and permanently lowers intensity; EP secures compliance where prevention is not (yet) feasible.

Fifth, we unpacked barriers to eco-innovation—which are, in effect, barriers to energy efficiency. We have divided them into internal and external to the firm. We have also underlined that finance is the modal constraint, especially for SMEs; but money rarely acts alone. Capabilities, managerial focus, data systems, policy certainty, and customer pull interact in a web of constraints. Without stable, outcome-based signals and the capabilities to respond, firms default to the minimum viable compliance—often EP—rather than the CP redesigns that bank durable savings.

Note

1 Not In My Backyard.

3 Eco-innovations, energy-efficiency gap and fiscal policy

Theoretical foundations

3.1 Introduction

Eco-innovations and energy efficiency are central to contemporary strategies of decarbonisation; yet, they remain systematically underprovided in market settings. As we saw in Chapter 2, firms fail to adopt the available profitable energy-saving technologies. Across sectors and countries, we can observe that firms do not implement energy-saving measures, even when they appear cost-effective ex ante. These solutions are frequently delayed, only partially implemented, or not undertaken at all (del Río et al., 2015; De Marchi, 2012; Popp, 2002).

This chapter builds the theoretical foundations linking eco-innovation, the energy-efficiency gap, and green fiscal policy. It frames intervention around market failures—especially the double externality problem—and reviews why market-based instruments can outperform command-and-control (CAC) regulation in aligning private incentives with environmental goals. It then explains how environmental taxes, subsidies, and tax credits reshape firms' cost–benefit calculations to support green technology development and diffusion, summarising evidence on their effects on eco-innovation and energy-efficient adoption. Finally, it motivates policy-mixes and sequencing and discusses distributional implications.

3.2 Double externality theory

According to Rennings (2000), energy-efficiency gap is the manifestation of the double externality problem. Rennings stated that the green technology diffusion is shaped simultaneously by two key externalities: "a knowledge externality" and an "environmental externality." The first one arises at the development stage, as green innovations are typically risky and expensive, which means innovators cannot fully appropriate the benefits of new knowledge once it is developed. Environmental externality, on the other hand, arises at the adoption stage, because, again the costs of diffusion are high, while the environmental benefits of adopting cleaner production technologies (or the

DOI: 10.4324/9781003712398-3

damages from dirty ones) are not fully internalised in the market prices, and so everyone benefits from the cleaner air, while it is only the innovator who bears the cost of the green technology adoption. Jaffe et al. (2005) restated the logic as a tale of two market failures—market failures in environmental quality, which interact with those in innovation and diffusion.

The joint presence of both justifies a coordinated policy mix rather than a single-instrument approach, since a single instrument addresses a single market failure (Tinbergen, 1952). Through environmental taxation, subsidies, and public expenditure, fiscal measures can address both the underpricing of environmental damage and the underinvestment in green innovation, while also influencing distributional outcomes and political feasibility (Acemoglu et al., 2012; Aghion et al., 2019). Thus, a coordinated, well-designed green fiscal policy architecture is not only crucial for governing the pace and direction of green technological change, but also affects firm productivity (Porter, 1991; Porter & van der Linde, 1995).[1] The European Commission's report reviewing empirical findings on environmental policy and firm productivity confirms that environmental policies may increase firm-level productivity, or at least not decrease it, but only under the right policy design (Tchorzewska, 2025a).

3.3 Market failures

Energy-efficiency shortfalls arise because markets rarely satisfy the conditions under which private choices coincide with the social optimum (Mas-Colell et al., 1995; Varian, 2014). Firms may waste energy through inefficient input choices, imperfect use of existing capital, or delayed adoption of superior technologies—contributing to the energy-efficiency gap (Bloom et al., 2010; Farrell, 1957). In practice, multiple market and non-market frictions distort incentives and help explain persistent underinvestment in eco-innovation and efficient technologies (Gerarden et al., 2017; Gillingham et al., 2009; Jaffe et al., 1994b).

Key failures include externalities (unpriced pollution damages plus unpriced benefits from early clean adoption), motivating Pigovian pricing and related instruments (Acemoglu et al., 2012; Baumol & Oates, 1988; Jaffe et al., 2005; Metcalf & Weisbach, 2012; Pigou, 1920; Popp, 2019); public-good knowledge and common-pool resources, which depress private Research and Development (R&D) and can misallocate shared resources without clear rights (Arrow, 1962; Fraser & Hone, 2003; Griliches, 1992; Nelson, 1959; Ostrom, 1990; Ostrom et al., 1994; Romer, 1990); information frictions that hinder comparison and raise transaction costs (Allcott & Greenstone, 2012; Gerarden et al., 2017; Gillingham et al., 2009); and behavioural biases (bounded rationality, present bias, status quo bias, and social norms) that pull decisions away from lifecycle–cost minimisation (Allcott, 2011; Kahneman et al., 1991; Laibson, 1997; Simon, 1955; Thaler & Sunstein, 2021). Finally, non-market frictions—such as installation disruption, learning costs, and uncertainty about performance, prices, or policy—can rationally deter adoption and must be separated from true market failures (Gillingham & Palmer, 2014; Hassett & Metcalf, 1993; Jaffe & Stavins, 1994a). Within this broader set, the double externality problem captures the joint presence of knowledge spillovers and environmental externalities in green innovation.

3.4 Market-based instruments versus command and control

Given these market and non-market failures, regulators may introduce energy and climate policies as corrective measures. From an economic perspective, we can see that these policies are justified when they help fix distorted price signals, close information gaps, and address broken incentives—so that private decisions about energy production, consumption, and technology choices move closer to what is best for society as a whole.

Energy and climate policies have different scopes and goals. Energy policies are nationally oriented, while climate policies are international. Energy policy targets the trilemma of security, affordability, and sustainability (World Energy Council, 2024), while climate policy focuses on mitigation and resilience. Since the objectives of those policies can conflict, instrument choice should be assessed jointly across both domains (OECD, 2007; Philibert, 2011). However, adoption of cleaner production (CP) technologies falls into both of those categories since they preserve energy while reducing pollution; while adoption of end-of-pipe (EP) technologies is related only to climate policy objectives, since they only reduce pollution at the end of the production pipe.

Regulator may choose between command-and-control (CAC) and/or market-based instruments (MBIs) (Baumol & Oates, 1988; Tietenberg & Lewis, 2023). CAC standards and mandates can guarantee minimum performance and are useful when monitoring is feasible or unacceptable technologies must be ruled out (Fujiwara, 2006; Stavins, 2003), but they are typically less cost-effective and weaker for innovation once compliance is reached (Jaffe et al., 2003; Milliman & Prince, 1989; Popp, 2002). MBIs—carbon/energy taxes, cap-and-trade, and price incentives—equalise marginal abatement costs and tend to deliver emissions reductions at lower cost while sustaining incentives for cleaner technologies (Milliman & Prince, 1989; Montgomery, 1972; Stavins, 2003; Tao et al., 2022). In the double externality framework, MBIs such as carbon taxes internalise environmental damages and strengthen demand-pull for eco-innovation (Jaffe et al., 2002, 2005; Popp, 2019), but they do not fix knowledge spillovers, so they must be complemented by innovation support within a policy-mix (Acemoglu et al., 2012; Arrow, 1962; Del Rio & Howlett, 2013; Fischer & Newell, 2008; Rogge & Reichardt, 2016; Tinbergen, 1952).

3.5 Green fiscal policies and their effects on eco-innovation

Green fiscal policies are a subset of market-based instruments. Alongside carbon/energy taxes and emissions trading, this category includes targeted subsidies and tax credits, accelerated depreciation, reduced value-added tax (VAT) for efficient equipment, the removal of environmentally harmful subsidies, and direct public spending on low-carbon infrastructure and R&D (Massetti & Bellon, 2022). Conceptually, pollution pricing mainly corrects the environmental externality, while targeted fiscal support is especially relevant for the knowledge and adoption margins emphasised by the double externality framework (Fischer & Newell, 2008; Jaffe et al., 2005; Popp, 2019).

Green fiscal policies shape eco-innovation through three channels. Demand-pull—carbon pricing raises the payoff to cleaner technologies and steers R&D towards low-carbon options (Jaffe et al., 2005; Popp, 2002). Technology-push—subsidies, R&D tax credits, and support for demonstration lower the private cost of knowledge creation with spillovers (Rennings, 2000); and risk-sharing—guarantees and stable, rules-based support reduce policy and market risk for high-fixed-cost investments (Aghion et al., 2016). Together, pricing and targeted support can accelerate diffusion by overcoming upfront costs and learning barriers (Bergek et al., 2008; Fischer & Newell, 2008; Nemet, 2006) and improve dynamic efficiency by reducing lock-in (Acemoglu et al., 2012; Arrow, 1962; Popp, 2019). But design also matters. Overly generous or volatile support can weaken incentives (or lead to opportune use), so credibility and alignment with long-run targets are crucial (Lehmann & Gawel, 2013; Rogge & Reichardt, 2016). Finally, drivers differ across eco-innovation types, motivating instrument- and mix-specific theory in the next section (García-Quevedo et al., 2022; Triguero et al., 2013).

3.5.1 Environmental taxes

Environmental taxes and carbon pricing are the canonical tools linking environmental policy to eco-innovation (Pigou, 1920). By putting a price on emissions or energy use, they shift relative prices between "dirty" and "clean" options and create demand-pull for low-emission technologies (Baumol & Oates, 1988; Jaffe et al., 2002; Pigou, 1920; Popp, 2019). In a static setting, a uniform tax (or permit price) leads each firm to abate until its marginal abatement cost equals the price, so reductions occur where they are cheapest—delivering a given target at minimum aggregate cost (Baumol & Oates, 1988).

When technology choice is endogenous, carbon pricing also reshapes innovation over time. Higher current and expected prices raise returns to emissions-saving R&D and cleaner capital, consistent with induced innovation and directed technical change (Acemoglu et al., 2012; Goulder & Schneider,

1999; Hicks, 1932; Popp, 2002, 2019). Empirically, stricter policies and higher energy prices are associated with more patenting in low-carbon and energy-efficient technologies (Aghion et al., 2016; Dechezleprêtre et al., 2017; Popp, 2002, 2019). Pricing also affects the choice between end-of-pipe and cleaner production options. Since every incremental reduction is rewarded, incentives tend to favour cleaner production technologies when they become the lower-cost margin (Frondel et al., 2007; Kemp & Pontoglio, 2011; Milliman & Prince, 1989).

This structure highlights several theoretical advantages of environmental taxes and carbon pricing. First, by directly embedding environmental damages into market prices, they regulate negative externalities through decentralised choices and are, in theory, more efficient at tipping investment decisions towards cleaner technologies than quantity or technology mandates that ignore cost heterogeneity (Baumol & Oates, 1988; Goulder & Parry, 2008; Tietenberg & Lewis, 2016). Second, they allow firms to use their own private information about technologies, processes, and abatement opportunities when choosing how to respond, which strengthens incentives to search for and implement innovative solutions rather than comply mechanically with prescriptive standards. Third, when revenues from environmental taxes are recycled efficiently into investment subsidies, lowering corporate income taxes, etc., they can correct externalities without increasing, and potentially even lowering, the overall welfare cost of taxation, thus increasing firm productivity and competitiveness (Yamazaki, 2017).

At the same time, there are important limitations. Accurate implementation requires robust measurement or estimation of emissions and damages; where monitoring is imperfect or marginal damages are uncertain, tax rates or caps may deviate from the optimum. Revenue from carbon pricing is uncertain and varies with economic conditions and behavioural responses, which complicate fiscal planning. Low levels of environmental taxations are also not effective at driving process eco-innovations (García-Quevedo et al., 2022, Tchórzewska et al., 2022), unless they are combined with subsidies or tax credits as a policy-mix (Tchórzewska et al., 2022). Hence, concerns are frequently raised about adverse competitiveness effects in trade-exposed, energy-intensive sectors as a result of environmental tax rates' inflation. Having said that, empirical work suggests that well-designed carbon pricing can coexist with strong performance, especially when innovation responses are considered, but short-run adjustment pressures and relocation risks remain a central part of the policy debate (Aghion et al., 2016; Aldy & Pizer, 2015).

Taken together, the theoretical foundations imply that well-designed environmental taxes and carbon pricing (i) internalise environmental damages and generate strong, technology-neutral demand-pull for low-carbon options; (ii) create continuous incentives for both end-of-pipe and CP responses, with a dynamic bias towards cost-reducing cleaner production; (iii) respect firms' informational advantages in choosing how to abate; and (iv) must be embedded in a broader fiscal and regulatory policy mix to address knowledge, financing, and competitiveness concerns (Popp, 2019). These mechanisms underpin subsequent empirical evaluations of how carbon pricing shapes eco-innovation trajectories in practice (Baumol & Oates, 1988; Fischer & Newell, 2008; Jaffe et al., 2002, 2003, 2005; Milliman & Prince, 1989; Popp, 2019; Rogge & Reichardt, 2016).

3.5.2 Environmental subsidies

Environmental subsidies are public transfers that lower the private cost of clean technologies or green R&D, helping correct market failures that impede eco-innovation and diffusion. Unlike pollution pricing, which raises the cost of carbon-intensive options, subsidies act by making cleaner alternatives cheaper and by directly supporting invention and uptake. Their rationale follows the double externality logic. When markets under-reward both green knowledge and environmental benefits, targeted support can move private returns closer to the social optimum (Arrow, 1962; Jaffe et al., 2005; Reichenbach & Requate, 2012). Evidence from China and other emerging markets suggests environmental and R&D subsidies can boost corporate green innovation, especially under financing constraints (Bai et al., 2019; Ma & Peng, 2025; Ma et al., 2023).

Properly designed subsidies operate through two main mechanisms. First, they create demand-pull for clean technologies by lowering acquisition and operating costs (e.g., through investment grants, feed-in tariffs, or production tax credits), which enlarge markets for green solutions, support scale economies, and accelerate learning-by-doing and network formation. This is particularly relevant where capital market imperfections are binding. By lowering upfront costs, subsidies and tax credits partially relax liquidity constraints and mitigate the effect of high-risk premia that would otherwise block investment, especially for SMEs and first-of-a-kind projects (Ang et al., 2017; Böhringer et al., 2014; Cecere et al., 2020; Chiappini et al., 2022; Fischer & Newell, 2008). Second, they provide technology-push by reducing the private cost and risk of R&D, pilots, and early deployment (R&D tax credits, demonstration funding), directly addressing underinvestment caused by knowledge spillovers (Jaffe et al., 2005; Shi & Zhou, 2024; Wang et al., 2025). Where the private profitability of new technologies is uncertain or highly state-contingent, investment-related tax credits and similar instruments share risk between firms and the state. They improve downside protection and raise expected net returns without requiring governments to pick individual projects.

The impact of subsidies on cleaner production versus end-of-pipe innovation depends critically on design (Frondel et al., 2007; García-Quevedo et al., 2022; Kemp & Pontoglio, 2011; Marino et al., 2024). As García-Quevedo et al. (2022) shows, only if they are designed well, they can be the most successful green fiscal tool at driving almost all types of superior production process eco-innovations, otherwise they might incentivise what is already required through regulations. They are also often more politically acceptable than explicit carbon taxes, because they are framed as support for clean investment rather than punitive charges, which can help build coalitions for transition.

These advantages come with significant trade-offs. First, subsidies impose a direct fiscal cost. Financing them requires taxes, borrowing, or the reallocation of public expenditure, so their net welfare effect depends on both environmental benefits, the opportunity cost of public funds; and offering funding may result in an opportune use of public. Second, if governments backs specific technologies rather than outcomes, there is a risk of technology lock-in and regulatory capture. Initially favoured or politically favoured options may continue to receive support even after they cease to be efficient, slowing the shift to superior alternatives (Eitan, 2023; Kozlova et al., 2023). Third, unlike pure price instruments, many subsidy schemes do not exploit firms' private information on abatement opportunities as effectively and the centralised design can misjudge relative costs, leading to over- or under-compensation. Fourth, there is a crowding-in versus crowding-out issue. Well-calibrated subsidies can leverage additional private investment, but overly generous or poorly targeted schemes may largely fund inframarginal projects that would have occurred anyway (free-riding), displace private finance, and weaken incentives to reduce costs (Hashemi et al., 2024; Marino et al., 2016).

3.5.3 Environmental investment tax credits

Environmental investment tax credits are green fiscal instruments that reduce a firm's tax liability in proportion to qualifying environmental investments (e.g., energy-efficient machinery, CP technologies, and pollution-control equipment). Like subsidies, they lower the user cost of capital and raise the net present value (NPV) of targeted investments. Their rationale also fits the double externality framework. By increasing private returns to investments that generate knowledge spillovers and environmental benefits, they narrow the gap between private and social incentives for adoption (Jaffe et al., 2005; Popp et al., 2009).

Compared with direct subsidies, tax credits operate through the tax system, reducing future revenue rather than requiring upfront outlays (OECD, 2025a). They also preserve firms' discretion within eligibility rules, leveraging decentralised information in investment choices (Hall & Jorgenson, 1967; Hassett & Hubbard, 2002; Lerche, 2025; Zwick & Mahon, 2017; Dechezleprêtre et al., 2023), and can be administratively simpler because they are embedded in routine tax filings (Böhringer et al., 2019). These features can make credits predictable and politically feasible (Goulder & Parry, 2008; Hall & Jorgenson, 1967; Hassett & Hubbard, 2002; Tchorzewska, 2025).

These properties translate into several advantages. Properly designed tax credits: (i) stimulate additional green investment by lowering the marginal cost of eligible capital; (ii) avoid large upfront cash transfers from the state, which may be politically and fiscally easier to implement than direct subsidies; (iii) can be implemented through general, rules-based provisions that are predictable for firms and simpler for administrations; and (iv) allow market forces to guide the allocation of support across projects and firms that meet environmental criteria, which, in principle, can enhance efficiency compared with heavily micro-managed grant schemes (Goulder & Parry, 2008; Hall & Jorgenson, 1967; Hassett & Hubbard, 2002; Tchorzewska, 2025). In settings where political resistance to explicit spending programmes is strong, or where governments aim to promote green investment while maintaining constraints on visible expenditures, investment tax credits can be an attractive design.

However, the same features also generate limitations that are directly relevant for eco-innovation. Because non-refundable tax credits are only valuable against positive tax liabilities, their effective incidence is skewed towards more profitable, established firms. Young, small, loss-making, or highly innovative firms with the strongest financing constraints may derive little or no immediate benefit unless provisions for refundability or carry-forward/carry-back are included. This creates a risk of regressive and uneven support. This is also supported by recent empirical findings, which show that when a tax credit is suddenly reintroduced, only the smallest firms (below 50 employees) increase green technology adoption as a result—having the biggest urgency in using that opportunity immediately (Tchorzewska, 2024). There is also a risk of inducing overinvestment or misallocation in favoured technologies or sectors if credit rates are too generous or eligibility too narrow, leading to distortions and potential crowding out of unsubsidised but socially desirable alternatives (Denes et al., 2023).

From a theoretical perspective, both subsidies and investment tax credits share the risk of inframarginal support and free-riding. Part of the fiscal cost may fund investments that would have occurred anyway (González & Pazó, 2008; Hashemi et al., 2024; Marino et al., 2016). Because tax credits are typically rules-based and less targeted, this risk can be significant unless environmental additionality and performance criteria are well specified. Moreover, unlike carbon pricing, tax credits do not inherently exploit firms' private information on least-cost abatement across all options; they operate only within the subset of investments that policymakers choose to privilege, which introduces an element of technology selection and associated risks of lock-in and regulatory capture (Bergek & Jacobsson, 2010; Kemp & Pontoglio, 2011; Rodrik, 2014). Overly technology-specific credits can entrench particular designs or fuels even when superior options emerge. Tax credits are also similar to subsidies in the sense that their design matters. If tax credits' eligibility is too loosely defined, such that it covers what is already required through environmental regulation, tax credits might finance through public money the inferior EP technologies (OECD, 2015). Having said that, there have been successful tax-credit scheme modifications, which through tighter definitions of the EI tax credit, decreased financing of inferior pollution-abating technologies, and increased superior CP technologies for the smallest firms (Tchorzewska, 2024). There is also empirical evidence that increasing proportionally the environmental investment tax credits increases the amount firms spend on superior CP technologies (Tchorzewska, 2025).

To conclude, environmental subsidies are powerful tools to overcome capital market failures, risk and information barriers, and underinvestment in green knowledge, and to support structural change, especially when paired with clear performance criteria. However, they must be integrated into a coherent policy-mix, ideally combined with carbon pricing that internalises environmental damages and with sunset and review mechanisms that limit fiscal burden, prevent lock-in, and maintain pressure for efficiency and innovation.

3.5.4 Policy-mixes

The innovation and transition policy literature has developed the logic of policy-mixes extensively, investigating complementarity, coherence, and interaction effects within instrument portfolios (Costantini et al., 2017; Flanagan et al., 2011; Lenihan et al., 2025a; Marino et al., 2016; Rogge & Reichardt, 2016; Uyarra et al., 2016). Applications focused explicitly on eco-innovation remain fewer, but converge on the idea that concurrent instruments can be more effective than isolated measures when well aligned (Greco et al., 2022; Veugelers, 2012; García-Quevedo et al., 2022; Tchórzewska et al., 2022).

Most green fiscal instruments target a single market failure: carbon taxes internalise pollution externalities, while subsidies address knowledge spillovers, following the principle of Tinbergen (1952) single market failure, single tool. Under the "double externality" logic, this motivates policy-mixes (Acemoglu et al., 2012). Hence, regulators layer carbon/energy pricing (or Emissions Trading System (ETS)) with innovation support, green subsidies or tax credits, and complementary regulatory or informational measures. In practice, addressing the double externality typically means combining environmental taxes with subsidies/tax credits for green adoption and innovation.

When green fiscal instruments operate together, they may be complementary, substitutive, rivalrous, or effectively independent. This makes careful evaluation essential for identifying policy-mixes that maximise complementarities and avoid policy-mixes, which are substitutes or rivalrous. The empirical eco-innovation literature aids us in assessment. For example, the literature shows that bundling general innovation support with environmental policy tends to strengthen process eco-innovations relative to stand-alone innovation measures (Greco et al., 2022). Environmental taxation also becomes more effective when paired with financial support—via tax credits or subsidies (García-Quevedo et al., 2022; Tchórzewska et al., 2022). Moreover, tax incentives and subsidies can play distinct yet mutually reinforcing roles across CP and EP technologies (del Río et al., 2016; García-Quevedo et al., 2022). The results from Tchórzewska et al. (2022) are particularly informative for policy design. The authors find that even modest environmental taxes can spur process eco-innovation when combined with public finance (subsidies and/or tax credits). However, this complementarity fades at higher tax levels, where sufficiently stringent taxation appears capable of inducing CP investment even without additional support.

In this book, a static policy-mix is therefore understood as a deliberately coordinated bundle of green fiscal instruments applied in the same period, designed so that: (i) pricing instruments correct environmental costs and create broad demand-pull; and (ii) subsidies, tax credits, and R&D support address financial and knowledge-related barriers. The effectiveness of such mixes depends on internal consistency. Instruments must be aligned in direction, timing, and doses, avoid contradictory incentives (e.g., simultaneous carbon pricing and fossil-fuel subsidies), and minimise redundancy and inframarginal transfers. Properly constructed, static policy-mixes provide a theoretical and practical framework for steering firms towards eco-innovation and cleaner production at lower overall social cost than any single instrument used in isolation.

3.5.5 *Sequential policy-mixes*

Sequential policy-mixes introduce time and ordering into the design of green fiscal policy-mixes. Instead of assuming that instruments are applied in a single moment in time, sequencing asks how the order of introduction of taxes, subsidies, standards, and other tools shapes firms' responses, amounts, and types of investment. A sequential policy-mix is thus a dynamic strategy in which earlier "stages" of policy are chosen to relax key barriers and build capabilities so that later, more demanding instruments become both effective and acceptable. This perspective extends beyond the static policy-mix literature and aligns with work on climate policy "ratcheting" and transition pathways, which shows that some policies function as enablers for stricter future interventions (Howlett, 2019; Leipprand et al., 2020; Pahle et al., 2018; Pakizer et al., 2023).

Eco-innovation is, as we have discussed earlier, constrained by multiple barriers: environmental externalities, knowledge spillovers, high upfront investment costs, financing frictions, technology risk, and information problems. These barriers differ in strength and nature, thus the effectiveness of an instrument depends on whether other, more binding obstacles have already been eased. A carbon tax introduced into an environment with severe financial constraints can fail to trigger green investment, because firms cannot fund the required technologies even if they become relatively more attractive. Conversely, early-stage support measures that reduce capital costs, de-risk new technologies, or build organisational capabilities can prepare firms to respond strongly once price-based instruments tighten. A successful sequence is one in which each policy step reduces at least one critical barrier without reinstating or worsening others, and thereby enables a move towards higher stringency and greater cost-effectiveness over time (Daugbjerg & Kay, 2020; Pahle et al., 2018).

Within this framework, green fiscal policies provide a natural "carrot first, stick second" architecture, as first shown by Tchorzewska et al. (2025) and consistent with the broader literature on policy sequencing and climate policy-mixes (Pahle et al., 2018; Rogge & Reichardt, 2016; Van den Bergh et al., 2021). This recent empirical paper using firm-level data shows that subsidies/tax credits first, environmental taxes second are sequential complements. Up-front instruments, such as investment subsidies or environmental tax credits, directly tackle financial and adoption barriers for green technologies, especially CP options with high fixed costs and strong learning potential. Once a critical base of capabilities and available capital is in place, environmental taxes or more stringent carbon pricing can be phased in or raised to internalise the environmental externality and sustain demand-pull for further innovation. The order matters because applying the "stick" in the absence of enabling conditions may induce compliance through cheap EP measures, output contraction, relocation, or plant exit rather than through transformative eco-innovation.

The same recent firm-level empirical paper provides evidence for how subsidies and tax credits are also sequential substitutes, in this case in any order. In this context, sequential substitutes are policy instruments where introducing one measure first reduces the additional impact of a second measure introduced later, or even makes it redundant or distortionary. For example, if generous investment subsidies or tax credits are maintained over a long period without adjustment, many firms will already have adopted available green technologies. A new or expanded subsidy introduced afterwards may then mainly finance projects that would have gone ahead anyway (inframarginal support/crowding-out), create windfall gains without stimulating extra innovation or additional emission reductions, or lock in earlier-generation technologies and slow down the shift towards more efficient or advanced options.

Recognising when instruments are sequential complements and when they become substitutes is therefore essential for designing effective policy pathways. A well-structured sequential policy-mix uses early-stage support to unlock investment and capabilities, then gradually tightens carbon pricing and streamlines subsidies, shifting from broad, generous support to more targeted, performance-based tools. This approach helps ensure that each new instrument adds genuine value, strengthens rather than offsets existing incentives, and maintains pressure for continuous eco-innovation and deeper decarbonisation over time.

3.6 Distributional implications of green fiscal policies

Just as green fiscal policies are efficiency tools, they are also distributional institutions that allocate the costs, risks, and rents of decarbonisation across sectors and firm types (Ohlendorf et al., 2021; Immervoll et al., 2023; Immervoll,

2024; Shang, 2023). The relevance of this aspect cannot be underrated. Perceived unfairness or capture can trigger political backlash and policy reversal, undermining the credibility that long-horizon R&D and capital investment require (Dabla-Norris et al., 2024; Douenne & Fabre, 2022; Maestre-Andrés et al., 2019; Patterson, 2025).

On the production side, carbon pricing shifts relative prices, redistributing burdens through output prices, demand shifts, and factor-price adjustments (Aldy & Pizer, 2015; Dechezleprêtre & Sato, 2017; Fullerton & Heutel, 2007). Yip (2018) finds short-run labour-market costs after a carbon tax—higher unemployment and lower wages—concentrated in energy-intensive industries, though unemployment returns to baseline after seven years. At the same time, predictable policy can reduce energy use without harming core firm outcomes. Martin et al. (2014) show the UK Climate Change Levy cut electricity use and energy intensity while leaving employment, revenue, productivity, and exit rates stable. What is more tax revenue recycling can even boost employment (Yamazaki, 2017), consistent with a Porter-type view that well-designed regulation can induce efficiency improvements (Porter, 1991).

Distributional issues also appear on the "pro-innovation" side. Subsidies, tax credits, and preferential finance will not broaden eco-innovation if access is uneven. When incentives are easier for incumbents with strong balance sheets, taxable profits, and administrative capacity, they can reinforce concentration and widen gaps between frontier and lagging firms (Dechezleprêtre et al., 2017). Design can counter this. Evidence from Italy shows sizeable effects of a general subsidy programme, with investment up 39% and employment up 17%, especially for smaller and younger firms (Cingano et al., 2023). Small firms also respond more strongly to R&D tax credits (Dechezlepretre et al., 2023), consistent with related fiscal evidence (Bronzini and Iachini, 2014; Criscuolo et al., 2019; Martinez-Ros & Kunapatarawong, 2019).

The distributive profile of green fiscal policy also operates through labour demand and skills. Green technologies typically require higher technical or university training, underscoring the need for reskilling capacity and local training systems to support firm-level adjustment (del Rio and Burguillo, 2009). Moreover, green jobs appear more volatile than aggregate employment, with stronger sensitivity to the business cycle and slower recoveries after downturns—raising concerns about job security and the stability of transition pathways for some workers and firms (Connolly et al., 2016; Ortega et al., 2015).

At the firm level, employment effects depend on the complementarity between technology and human capital (Cecere & Mazzanti, 2017; Horbach & Rennings, 2013). Eco-innovations typically raise demand for skilled labour needed to implement new technologies and organisational change (Aldieri et al., 2019; Rennings et al., 2004). Evidence suggests greener, more innovative firms can experience stronger employment growth. This is shown for German firms (Horbach & Rennings, 2013) and for environmental patenting in Italy (Gagliardi et al., 2016). Importantly, impacts differ by innovation type. CP innovations are linked to positive employment effects, while (EP innovations are often insignificant; similar patterns are found for Spain, with stronger gains from voluntary than compliance-driven eco-innovation (Biggi et al., 2023; Zhang et al., 2024). Using Spanish firm microdata, del Río et al. (2025) find positive effects of cleaner production on green jobs, with stronger impacts in the long run than the short run.

Job quality arising from green jobs, however, cannot be assumed. Moreira et al. (2018), studying Portugal, find that green jobs receive less occupational health and safety coverage and experience higher incidence and severity of workplace accidents, often being filled by less qualified workers. For firms, this implies that transition strategies oriented towards employment creation must also integrate training, protection, and organisational capability—not merely headcounts.

Eco-innovation also interacts with finance by shifting banks' portfolios and transition-risk exposure (Nguyen, 2025); adoption in adjacent domains can reduce bank and systemic risk on balance (Hryckiewicz et al., 2023). Finally, perceived unfairness or instability increases political contestation and policy volatility, shortening investment horizons and slowing eco-innovation (Baranzini & Carattini, 2017; Carattini et al., 2018; Klenert et al., 2018).

3.7 Conclusions

This chapter clarified why eco-innovations and energy-efficient technologies are systematically underprovided in unregulated markets, highlighting the joint role of environmental externalities, knowledge spillovers, internal inefficiencies, financing frictions, etc. The double externality framework provides the central lens. Green innovation is penalised twice, at the innovation and adoption margins, so that relying on market forces alone cannot deliver a socially efficient pace or direction of technological change.

On this basis, the chapter has defined green fiscal policy as a core component of the corrective architecture. It outlined the theoretical effects of environmental taxes and carbon pricing, green subsidies, environmental investment tax credits, and their static and sequential policy-mixes on green technology adoption, distinguishing cleaner production from EP responses. It has also shown that instrument choice, design, and sequencing matter. Policies interact, some combinations are complementary, others redundant or distortionary, and the timing of "carrots" and "sticks" influences whether firms adjust through genuine eco-innovation or through short-term, low-effort compliance. Finally, the discussion of distributional implications established that incidence is integral to dynamic efficiency and policy credibility; poorly designed green fiscal measures can undermine political support and weaken the very innovation incentives they are meant to strengthen.

The following chapters use this framework to organise and assess the modern empirical literature on individual green fiscal instruments and their policy-mixes. Each instrument is examined against the criteria derived here. Its effectiveness in correcting relevant market failures thus incentivising green technology adoption and its interaction with other policies in static and sequential mixes. This transition from theory to evidence allows a disciplined evaluation of which green fiscal policies work, for whom, under what conditions, and with what implications for a cost-effective and socially robust low-carbon transition.

Note

1 Porter's hypothesis (1995) says that strict but well-designed environmental regulation can stimulate innovation that more than offsets compliance costs, making firms more productive and competitive rather than less.

4 Modern empirical evaluations of individual green fiscal policies

4.1 Introduction

This chapter moves from theory to modern ex-post empirical modelling. The previous discussion developed a conceptual case for green fiscal policies. We discussed how taxes, subsidies, tax credits, and their combinations can correct market failures, support eco-innovation, and shape the pace and direction of technological change. We now turn to more practical questions. How should we model them empirically? And what do we actually know about how these instruments perform in the real world individually?

Our focus is on four closely linked research questions. First, which green fiscal instruments are effective in encouraging firms to adopt green technologies, especially energy-efficient? Two, does the marginal increase in the instrument dose increase cleaner-production (CP) or end-of-pipe (EP) technologies more? Three, what minimum level or "dose" of taxation, subsidy, or support is needed to induce meaningful change, rather than marginal adjustments? And fourth, to what extent can existing instruments be redesigned—through changes in targeting, conditionality, or structure—to better support energy-efficient and low-carbon technologies?

Answering these questions requires modern empirical methods that rely on a set of identification strategies—fixed-effects models, categorical treatment matching, difference-in-differences (DiD) designs, instrumental variables (IVs), and regression discontinuity designs—to isolate the causal impact of specific policies from other forces shaping investment, innovation, and performance. Each approach brings its own strengths, limitations, and assumptions, and these methodological choices directly affect how confidently we can speak about the effectiveness, efficiency, and design of green fiscal instruments.

4.2 Which green fiscal instruments work best for adoption of green technologies?

The following sections review what recent empirical work tells us about the effectiveness of major green fiscal instruments in driving the adoption of

DOI: 10.4324/9781003712398-4

low-carbon and energy-efficient technologies. We are organising by method, but by doing that, we also organise by the four main policy questions: (1) effectiveness, (2) proportional increase of a policy instrument, (3) minimum effective intensity/dose, and (4) redesigning of existing green fiscal policies, thus showing which methodologies can help us in evaluating which policy question. Along the way, we highlight how different identification strategies underpin the results. The aim is to give a clear, policy-relevant picture of "what works," while signalling where findings are robust and where they remain contested.

4.2.1 Fixed-effects models

A large empirical literature has examined what drives firms to adopt cleaner technologies and improve energy efficiency (del Río et al. 2016; Horbach et al. 2012; Jaffe & Palmer, 1997; Jaffe et al., 2002; Kerr & Newell, 2003; Lilliestam et al.,2021; Oussama and Oluyede, 2022; Requate, 2005). Those studies typically evaluate the drivers of eco-innovations. Distinguishing between CP and EP technologies (Frondel et al., 2007), they also underline that since eco-innovations have different characteristics—they also have different drivers (De Marchi, 2012; Haller and Murphy, 2012; Triguero et al., 2013). A prominent example of such paper is the paper by García-Quevedo et al. (2022), which investigates environmental policy tools and organisational behaviour with a panel dataset 14,528 firm–year observations for Spanish manufacturing firms between 2008 and 2014. The authors compare green fiscal policy tools and organisational behaviour indicators, more specifically: environmental taxes, subsidies for green investment and environmental investment tax credits against green employees, and environmental certifications. Their empirical strategy looks as follows:

$$\begin{aligned} \ln\_ECOINN_{it} = \beta_1 \ln\_ECOINN_{it-1} + \beta_2 dT_{it} + \beta_3 dS_{it} + \beta_4 dTC_{it} \\ + \beta_5 dGE_{it} + \beta_6 d\mathrm{E}C_{it} + \beta_7 Size_{it} + \alpha_i + \alpha_s + \alpha_t + \epsilon_{it} \end{aligned} \tag{4.1}$$

In the model specification (4.1), $\ln\_ECOIN_{i,t}$ denotes the natural logarithm of firm i's expenditure on eco-innovation in year t, including either CP or EP technologies. The lagged term $\ln\_ECOIN_{i,t-1}$ captures path dependence, since firms that invested in eco-innovation in the past are more likely to continue doing so. The dummy variable $dT_{i,t}$ indicates whether firm i pays environmental taxes in year t (thus operates in an autonomous community that has an environmental tax in place in year t); $dS_{i,t}$ equals 1 if the firm received a subsidy for green technology adoption in that year and $dTC_{i,t}$ captures the use of a tax credit on green technology investment in the corresponding fiscal year. $dGE_{i,t}$ records whether the firm employs staff dedicated to environmental protection activities, while $dEC_{i,t}$ indicates whether the firm holds environmental certifications. Firm size is included as a standard control.

The model specification further incorporates firm fixed effects (α_i) to control for unobserved, time-invariant characteristics at the firm level (such as managerial quality, corporate culture, or persistent technological capabilities), thereby mitigating bias from firms' self-selection into policies or green strategies. Sector fixed effects (α_s) account for systematic differences across industries (such as typical innovation intensity or regulatory exposure constant over time), and year fixed effects (α_t) capture shocks common to all firms each year (such as macroeconomic conditions, national policy shifts, or energy price trends). Standard errors are clustered at the firm level to account for serial correlation.

This specification has several attractive features. First, it acknowledges that eco-innovation is path dependent rather than a one-off decision. Second, it directly links multiple policy instruments—taxes, subsidies, and tax credits—to eco-innovation spending, allowing a comparative assessment of their marginal associations within a unified framework. It does so with the use of dummy variables, to focus on the extensive margin. Third, the inclusion of firm, sector, and year fixed effects provides a relatively strong structure for handling unobserved heterogeneity, improving the credibility of within-firm estimates, and helping to control for stable selection effects. Fourth, the use of logged eco-innovation expenditure (for positive values) allows coefficients to be interpreted in approximate percentage terms, which is intuitive for policy discussions.

At the same time, several limitations should be recognised. While the authors use dummy variables to limit the issue of endogeneity, it is still likely to be present within the policy variables. Subsidies and tax credits are unlikely to be randomly assigned. In the end, more innovative, better-connected, or more capable firms may be both more likely to receive support and to invest in eco-innovation. Similarly, even though environmental taxes are introduced in Spain at the regional level, and hence are highly heterogeneous, it might be that those regions are already on specific economic or environmental trajectories. With only fixed effects and contemporaneous dummies, the model cannot fully rule out reverse causality or time-varying confounders, so estimates are best seen as conditional correlations unless supported by stronger identification (e.g., DiD, IV, RDD).

Having said that, in the absence of a stronger identification strategy, the authors undertake a series of robustness checks to test the stability of their findings. They re-estimate the model on a balanced panel and across alternative time windows. They also replace eco-innovation expenditure with a related outcome—private environmental Research and Development (R&D)—as if placebo outcome. Since subsidies are provided for adoption of green technologies, they should not be successful at increasing private environmental R&D.

Authors also employ several alternative estimation approaches. A random-effects Tobit model is used to account for censoring among non-investing firms. A fixed-effects logit specification allows for a non-linear relationship by modelling the probability of undertaking eco-innovation rather than its level. Finally, an Arellano–Bond dynamic panel estimator is applied to better address persistence in eco-innovation and potential bias arising from the inclusion of lagged dependent variables. These sensitivity analyses increase confidence that the main results are not driven by modelling choices or sample peculiarities, even if they do not fully resolve all identification concerns.

Taken together, equation (4.1) is a sensible baseline specification. It is transparent, grounded in theory, and well suited for exploratory analysis and within-firm comparisons to study the effectiveness of implementation of different green fiscal policies (the extensive margin more specifically). But we need to keep in mind that its results should be interpreted cautiously and, ideally, complemented by designs that better address endogeneity, dynamics, and possibly even the intensive margins—such as policy shocks in a DiD framework, instrumental variables for policy exposure, or threshold-based strategies—especially if the goal is to draw strong causal conclusions about the effectiveness of specific green fiscal instruments.

Table 4.1 presents the main results from the paper by García-Quevedo et al. (2022). Their empirical results suggest that environmental taxes in

Table 4.1 Main results: Fixed-effects regression estimations for log investment in CP, CPair, CPenc, EP, and EPair

	lnCP (1)	*lnCP* (2)	*lnCPair* (3)	*lnCPenc* (4)	*lnEP* (5)	*lnEP* (6)	*lnEPair* (7)
L.1	−0.04***	−0.03***	0.01	0.01	−0.05***	−0.05***	−0.02***
	(0.01)	(0.01)	(0.00)	(0.01)	(0.01)	(0.01)	(0.01)
dtax	0.27	0.27	0.24	0.43**	0.12	0.12	0.14
	(0.28)	(0.28)	(0.21)	(0.21)	(0.28)	(0.28)	(0.18)
dsub	1.55***	1.52***	0.62*	1.05***	1.25***	1.25***	0.77**
	(0.46)	(0.46)	(0.36)	(0.36)	(0.41)	(0.41)	(0.33)
dtcred	3.67***	3.66***	2.19***	0.27	0.87	0.86	1.08**
	(0.57)	(0.57)	(0.54)	(0.51)	(0.54)	(0.54)	(0.48)
dgreen_empl	1.04***	1.02***	0.56**	0.68***	1.35***	1.39***	0.74***
	(0.36)	(0.36)	(0.29)	(0.18)	(0.36)	(0.35)	(0.21)
denv_cert	0.62**	0.62*	0.07	0.45*	0.01	−0.02	0.01
	(0.32)	(0.32)	(0.24)	(0.24)	(0.29)	(0.29)	(0.18)
size dummies	×	×	×	×	×	×	×
time FE	×	×	×	×	×	×	×
firm FE	×	×	×	×	×	×	×
sector FE		×	×	×		×	×
N	14,528	14,528	14,528	14,528	14,528	14,528	14,528
F stat	11.44				26.61		
Prob >F	0.00				0.00		

(*Source*: García-Quevedo et al., 2022)

Note: All standard errors are clustered at the firm level. ***, **, and * denote significance at the 99% level, 95% level, and 90% level, respectively. Mean Variance Inflation Factor (VIF) is equal to 8.18. All the models include time, firm, and sector fixed effects, except for models 1, 5, 6, and 9, which do not include sector fixed effects.

Spain do not significantly stimulate additional investment in either CP or EP technologies, except for technologies that are energy-efficient (as can be seen in model 4). By contrast, both investment subsidies and tax credits are rather consistently associated with higher levels of green technology adoption among Spanish manufacturing firms. In line with the theoretical expectation that process-integrated solutions are more transformative, the estimated effects are generally stronger for CP technologies than for add-on abatement equipment. Notably, tax credits appear particularly effective in this regard. Their estimated impact on CP investment is roughly twice as large as that of subsidies (models 1–3), indicating that well-designed fiscal incentives at the firm level can play a central role in shifting resources towards deeper, process-based decarbonisation. This book answers its first research question by arguing that green fiscal policies can be effective at inducing green technology adoption—especially energy-efficient solutions—under the right policy design.

4.2.2 Instrumental-variable approach

As we have previously mentioned, while fixed-effects models are great tools to compare several policy instruments within a single consistent framework, there can be doubts whether the effects really capture causality, and thus the results should be taken with caution. It is best to treat them as strong correlations. In the following section, we shall discover how economists use IV approach in combination with, for example, fixed-effects models to investigate the causal effect of a carbon tax (Martin et al. 2014) and of an environmental investment tax credit (Tchorzewska, 2025b).

In the study of Martin et al. (2014), the impact of the UK Climate Change Levy is identified by comparing plants that pay the full tax rate with plants that receive an 80% discount through participation in Climate Change Agreements (CCAs), using plant-level panel data. The authors begin from a fixed-effects logic in which energy and productivity-related outcomes are related to tax exposure while controlling for standard covariates and absorbing plant-specific and year-specific factors. But they treat this baseline comparison as potentially contaminated by three features of the policy environment. The "control" group is not fully untreated because CCA plants face separate targets, participation in CCAs is voluntary and limited to eligible plants (so selection is a concern), and the tax effect may vary across plants. To tighten identification, they first-difference the panel to remove time-invariant unobserved plant characteristics—traits such as technology, size, or underlying energy intensity that might jointly shape both outcomes and programme participation—yet, they acknowledge that differencing alone cannot rule out sorting based on anticipated future changes in energy use. They therefore add an IV layer that exploits exogenous eligibility rules for CCA participation as a source of variation in effective tax treatment, estimating two-stage least squares in first differences and complementing this with reduced-form ("intent-to-treat") estimates that relate outcomes directly to eligibility. The resulting design—with fixed-effects logic and eligibility-based instrumental variable—aims to recover a credible causal estimate of the levy's effect while explicitly addressing non-random participation and the partially treated nature of the comparison group. Although, in the study the outcome variables include energy use, intensity, employment, revenues, and exits rather than green technology adoption, the same empirical architecture can be straightforwardly repurposed to study adoption of low-carbon and, especially, energy-efficient solutions under green fiscal policy.

Similarly, Tchorzewska (2025b) uses the IV approach in combination with DiD fixed-effects model to examine the proportional effect of an environmental investment tax credit on green technology adoption among Spanish manufacturing firms (IV is widely adopted to study R&D tax credits; Czarnitzki & Hottenrott, 2011; Gelabert et al., 2009; Gonzalez et al., 2005; Wallsten, 2000). In this case, IV strategy allows also for investigation of the intensive margin.

Institutional setting is also an important factor here for identification purposes. The Spanish Environmental Investment (EI) Tax Credit existed in the Spanish Corporate Income Tax from the 1996 at the rate of 10% of the total investment cost. In 2006, the government decided to slowly phase out the tax credit by 2% each year until its full phase-out in 2011. However, unexpectedly in March 2011, the Spanish government decided to reintroduce the tax credit for a few more years at a stable rate of 8% (shown in Figure 4.1 and Table 4.2).

The paper by Tchorzewska (2025b) exploits the policy changes between 2008 and 2014, in particular, the fact that the statutory tax-credit rate varied over time (Table 4.2). The key idea is to use the tax-credit rate in 2008 as an instrument for firms' effective tax-credit exposure in later years. The 2008 rate is strongly correlated with subsequent use and intensity of the tax credit, but—by construction—does not directly determine the scale of green technology

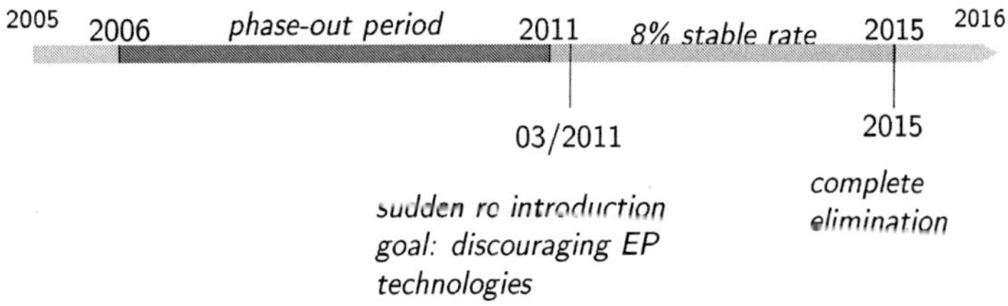

Figure 4.1 The changes in the Environmental Investment (EI) tax credit over the years (*Source*: self-made)

Table 4.2 EI tax credit rates—Planned versus actual

Year	*2008 (%)*	*2009 (%)*	*2010 (%)*	*2011 (%)*	*2012 (%)*	*2013 (%)*	*2014 (%)*
Planned rate	6	4	2	0	0	0	0
Actual rate	6	4	2	8	8	8	8

(*Source*: Tchorzewska, 2025b)

adoption in later periods. This design allows the author to isolate the causal impact of tax-credit generosity on firms' adoption decisions. The first and second stages of the model look as follows:

$$\ln\_taxcredit_{it} = \beta_0 + \beta_1 taxcred2008_i + \beta_2 dpost2011_t + \delta\left(taxcred2008 * post2011\right)_{it} + \theta X_{it} + \alpha_i + \alpha_t + \epsilon_{it} \tag{4.2}$$

$$\ln\_outcome_{it} = \varphi_0 + \varphi_1 \ln\_taxcredit_{it} + \rho X_{it} + \alpha_i + \alpha_t + \epsilon_{it} \tag{4.3}$$

In the first-stage specification (4.2), the study models firms' effective exposure to the policy by regressing the logarithm of the tax credit on three main elements: the amount of the tax credit received in 2008, a post-2011 indicator (dummy variable), and their interaction. The model includes also control variables, time- and year-fixed effects; and the error terms are clustered at the firm level to account for serial correlation. This provides a predicted (instrumented) measure of tax-credit intensity that reflects how pre-policy differences translate into the later treatment. In the second stage, those fitted values are used in place of the observed tax credit to estimate its impact on firms' behaviour (φ_1). Similarly to (4.2), specification (4.3) also includes typical firm-level control variables, firm- and year-fixed effects; and standard errors are clustered at the firm level. The model is not only used with other productivity-related dependent variables, partially as robustness checks, but also to investigate whether indirect effects are present, for example, total employment (lnsize), green employment (lngrsize), green wages (lngrsalary), and green private R&D (lngrRD).

The key identification assumption in this model is that the initial 2008 tax-credit amount is plausibly exogenous with respect to subsequent green investment trajectories, not all firms invest every year, and conditional on controls, cross-firm variation in the 2008 credit captures quasi-random differences in baseline eligibility and use, rather than forward-looking choices about later green technology adoption. This is captured by Figure 4.2 presenting the relationship between the instrument and the tax-credit amount between the years 2011 and 2014.

From a methodological point of view, the strategies used in Martin et al. (2014) and Tchorzewska (2025b) illustrate the main strengths and weaknesses

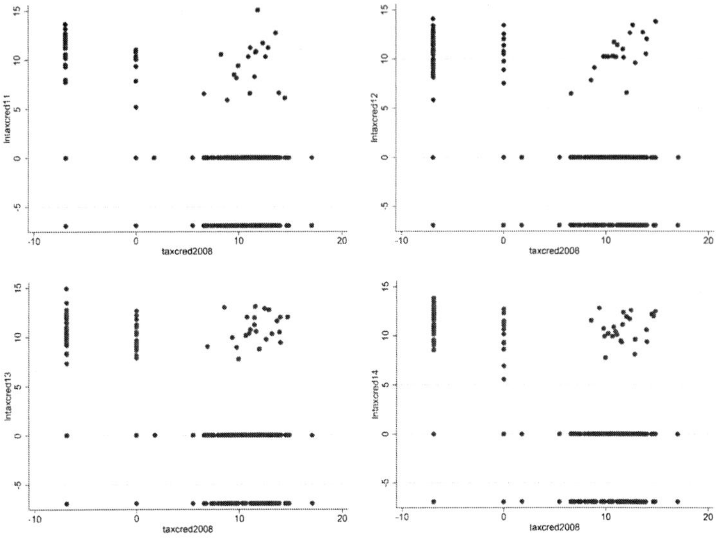

Figure 4.2 The relationship between the instrument and the tax-credit amount between the years 2011 and 2014

(*Source*: Tchorzewska, 2025b)

of combining firm-level panel data with IVs (often in a DiD-style setting) for evaluating green fiscal policies. On the positive side, these designs move beyond simple fixed-effects models by exploiting plausibly exogenous sources of variation in policy exposure. In the UK case, eligibility rules for CCAs provide differential access to reduced tax rates; in the Spanish case, historically determined tax-credit levels and subsequent reforms generate quasi-experimental variation in effective support intensity. In both settings, the IV approach helps to correct for non-random selection into treatment. Firms do not receive full taxes or amount of tax credit by accident—and for the fact that more energy-intensive or more innovative firms may be systematically more likely to participate in favourable schemes. Using panel data and fixed effects further purges time-invariant unobserved characteristics, so that identification is driven by changes over time within the same firms. When the underlying assumptions hold, this combination delivers a credible estimate of the causal effect at the margin.

For policymakers, if IV is chosen well—it is both exogeneous to the outcome and relevant to the instrumented variable itself, this is a major advantage. These strategies yield parameters that are directly interpretable in policy terms (e.g., "what happens to adoption if we introduce another tax credit, tighten eligibility, reduce discounts, or increase the tax credit rate?"), and they can be applied consistently across multiple outcomes—energy use, emissions, productivity, and, where data permit, eco-innovation indicators. They show how real-world institutional features (eligibility rules, phased reforms, step-wise changes in rates) can be turned into quasi-experiments rather than treated as technical detail.

However, there are also important limitations that matter especially when extending such approaches to eco-innovation. First, everything hinges on the validity of the instrument (relevance and exogeneity). Eligibility rules or past tax-credit levels must affect outcomes only through the policy channel of interest. If these rules are correlated with other supports, regulatory pressure, or firms' strategic choices, the exclusion restriction may be violated and the estimates biased. Second, IV strategies typically identify a local average treatment effect for firms whose behaviour is altered by the instrument ("compliers"). That effect may differ from the average response across all firms, particularly for eco-innovation, where large pioneers and smaller followers may react very differently to the same fiscal signal.

In sum, IV-based strategies built on institutional rules or historical policy parameters are among the most powerful tools currently available for causal evaluation of green fiscal policies. They are especially well suited where clear eligibility criteria, phased reforms, or discrete policy shocks exist. Yet, for eco-innovation analysis, they should be applied with careful attention to instrument validity, interpretation of local effects, and the dynamic nature of technology adoption. Ideally, they should complement, rather than replace, other designs such as rich DiD specifications, RDD at policy thresholds, and detailed micro-data on specific CP and EP technologies (Table 4.3).

Regarding the empirical results related to green fiscal policy and green technology adoption, we will focus on Tchorzewska (2025b), since as we

Table 4.3 The main results of a proportional effect of the EI tax credit on green technology adoption

	(1) *lnCP*	(2) *lnCPair*	(3) *lnCPenc*	(4) *lnEP*	(5) *lnEPair*
lntaxcredit	0.305***	1.391***	0.407**	0.208***	0.918***
	(0.071)	(0.290)	(0.173)	(0.069)	(0.264)
lnsize	0.619***	0.968***	1.425***	0.590***	0.648***
	(0.071)	(0.157)	(0.130)	(0.078)	(0.134)
Observations	2,833	9,972	9,972	1,991	9,972
R-squared	0.000	0.000	0.037	0.095	0.000

(*Source*: Tchorzewska, 2025b)

Note: Each coefficient is estimated from different regression following the IV specification. The dependent variables are the amount in the log of equipment investment. Those measures are used both for investment in Cleaner Production (CP) and End-of-Pipe (EP) technologies. Additional controls are firm size, sector, and year dummies. Standard errors in parentheses are clustered at the firm level. *** $p < 0.01$, ** $p < 0.05$, and * $p < 0.1$.

mentioned Martin et al. (2014) do not investigate green technology adoption but other firm-level productivity measures. The estimates indicate that more generous environmental investment tax credits are associated with higher spending on CP technologies, thus those technologies that are more capital-intensive and transformative. The strongest response is found for investments in CP technologies targeting air pollution (lnCPair), suggesting that firms use additional fiscal space to undertake more ambitious, process-integrated upgrades rather than only marginal EP adjustments. To test the robustness of these findings, the author implements an alternative IV specification that also uses lagged tax-credit receipts as an instrument for current exposure to a tax credit. The results remain broadly consistent across these formulations, strengthening the interpretation that higher effective tax-credit rates causally support deeper, cleaner production investments.

Thus, this book answers its second research question by arguing that green fiscal policies have proportional effects at inducing green technology adoption—especially energy-efficient solutions.

4.3 How much is enough? The "dose" of green fiscal incentives

Once we have established whether a green fiscal policy is effective on average, and that increasing the marginal intensity increases green technology adoption, the next question is at what intensity does it work best? Meaning at what *dose* does it stimulate green technology adoption and which type of green technology adoption? As we know, this "dose" dimension is particularly important for fiscal instruments. For environmental taxes and carbon pricing, setting the rate too low yields little behavioural change; firms simply absorb the cost and continue with existing technologies. But setting it too high risks undermining firm productivity, international competitiveness, and in some cases even plant survival—especially in trade-exposed, energy-intensive sectors (Dechezleprêtre et al., 2018). The policy challenge is to identify the minimum carbon price that meaningfully accelerates green technology adoption without imposing disproportionate adjustment costs.

A similar calibration problem arises for investment subsidies and tax credits. These instruments are financed from public resources and thus carry an opportunity cost. If support levels are too modest, they will not overcome liquidity constraints, risk perceptions, or payback barriers, and additional green investment will remain limited. If they are overly generous, they risk subsidising projects that would have proceeded anyway, crowding out private finance and inflating fiscal costs without commensurate environmental or innovation benefits. In the case of tax incentives, overly generous support can create windfall profits for firms rather than additional environmental effort, implying a risk of wasting public resources (Arguedas & van Soest, 2009). In both cases, a careful empirical analysis of dose–response relationships is essential to design instruments that are strong enough to crowd in green investment, but not so strong that they mainly fund inframarginal or non-additional projects.

4.3.1 Categorical treatment matching

A particularly useful methodology that could be used here is the recently proposed categorical treatment matching by Marino et al. (2016) to study R&D tax credits on general innovation and even more recently adapted by Tchórzewska et al. (2022) for green fiscal policies and green technology uptake specifically. We shall focus on the publication of Tchórzewska et al. (2022), which investigates the heterogeneous effects of different doses of environmental taxes on green technology investment levels.

The starting point is a conventional propensity score matching (PSM) setup. Firms are classified as treated if they pay an environmental tax and untreated if they do not. As we mentioned in Spain, certain regions have implemented environmental taxes at different rates, while others did not, which led to substantial rather exogeneous heterogeneity. The probability of treatment is modelled as a function of pre-treatment characteristics ($t - 1$), such as firm size, sector, and lagged investments in CP, EP technologies, and other green expenditures; and treated and untreated firms are matched on this propensity score. Under the standard assumptions of conditional independence and common support, this allows estimation of the average effect of being taxed on subsequent green investment, while reducing bias from observable differences between taxed and untaxed firms. Additionally, in this particular context, the methodology is well suited to the institutional setting, since self-selection into treatment is mitigated by limited mobility across autonomous communities. Exposure is largely determined by local tax policy rather than firms' location choices.

However, a binary specification may mask substantial heterogeneity across tax levels and cannot capture the possibility that low levels of taxation are ineffective, while higher levels create meaningful incentives. To address this, Tchórzewska et al. (2022) extend the analysis by grouping firms into several tax-intensity categories. Practically, they divide the distribution of environmental tax payments into terciles and distinguish four mutually exclusive groups: non-payers (untreated), and low, medium, and high environmental tax payers. This data-driven classification avoids arbitrary policy cut-offs and, in robustness checks, is replicated using tax payments per employee to ensure that results are not purely size-driven. The number of categories is deliberately limited, more groups would thin out the sample in each cell, weaken statistical power, and risk the loss of common support.

Categorical treatment matching then estimates, for each firm, the probability of belonging to each tax-intensity category given its pre-treatment characteristics and matches firms with similar scores across categories. This enables systematic comparisons not only between taxed and untaxed firms, but also between different levels of taxation (e.g., high vs. medium, medium vs. low)—thus also controlling for self-selection into general treatment. Under the usual assumptions, differences in eco-innovation outcomes between matched firms can be interpreted as the effect of moving from one "dose" of environmental taxation to another. To ensure high-quality matches, the authors employ a caliper rule restricting matches to firms with closely aligned propensity scores and they also check robustness using alternative matching algorithms.

Categorical treatment matching offers several strengths for evaluating green fiscal policies and their impact on eco-innovation. Firstly, it captures intensity, not just presence. Secondly, it allows for flexible comparison across multiple treatment levels. Unlike standard binary PSM, this method allows comparisons between multiple tax brackets (low vs. medium, medium vs. high, high vs. zero), helping uncover non-linearities and thresholds in firms' responses. Thirdly, it is transparent and relatively intuitive. Grouping firms into ordered categories (e.g., terciles) is easy to explain and defend, particularly when based on the distribution rather than subjective cut-offs. Fourthly, it provides a less parametric structure than regression-based dose–response. Matching relies less on functional-form assumptions about how taxation relates to adoption. This can be attractive when eco-innovation responses are believed to be non-linear or heterogeneous. Lastly, it is adaptable across instruments. The same logic can be applied to subsidy rates, tax-credit generosity, or support intensity, making it a versatile tool in comparative evaluations of green fiscal instruments.

At the same time, categorical treatment matching has important limitations that should temper its use and interpretation. Firstly, a central limitation of propensity score matching, as pointed out by Guerzoni and Raiteri (2015), is that it relies on observables alone (unconfoundedness). The method assumes that, conditional on observed characteristics, assignment to tax-intensity categories is as good as random. If unobserved factors—such as management quality, environmental culture, or latent innovation capacity—influence both tax payments and eco-innovation, estimates may still be biased. Lastly, categorical treatment matching has yet another limitation—common support and sample size constraints. As the number of categories increases, it becomes harder to find good matches across groups. In sparse or skewed samples, this can lead to dropping many observations, reducing precision, and potentially limiting external validity. Thus, large datasets are encouraged for this type of investigation.

The contribution of Tchórzewska et al. (2022) addresses those concerns in a few ways. Firstly, it moves beyond this binary view and uses categorical treatment matching to study the dose–response relationship between environmental taxation and eco-innovation. By doing so, it can compare firms between different intensities of treatment and—thus to a certain point controlling for self-selection into treatment itself. Secondly, following Marino et al. (2016) authors tried to tackle the existing bias by addressing sources of unobserved heterogeneity. More specifically, the authors try to control for firm-specific time-invariant characteristics by using outcome variables in first differences. But additionally, the authors also perform matching between the treated and control groups in each observational year based on pre-treatment characteristics to ensure that comparisons include all observable within-firm changes occurring on an annual basis.

Overall, however, categorical treatment matching is a useful intermediate technique, more informative than simple treated/untreated comparisons and more transparent than heavily parameterised non-linear models, but still dependent on strong assumptions about observables and sample structure. In the context of eco-innovation, its real value lies in highlighting heterogeneity in responses to different policy intensities—insights that can then be cross-validated with complementary approaches such as continuous dose–response models, DiD with varying treatment intensities, or IV strategies based on exogenous policy shifts.

With regards to results and policy implications, Tchórzewska et al. (2022) carry out this analysis for both environmental taxation and public funding (subsidies and tax credits for investment aggregated together). Table 4.4 provides results for environmental taxation alone.

The categorical treatment matching results in Table 4.4 sheds light on how different intensities of environmental taxation translate into firms' investment in eco-innovation. The analysis focuses on investment in cleaner production technologies (lnCP) and investment in end-of-pipe technologies (lnEP)—the version in the paper includes also lnCP per capita and lnEP per

Table 4.4 Results from categorical treatment matching, the effect of environmental taxation on eco-innovation

	lnCP			*lnEP*		
	No tax	**Small**	**Medium**	**No tax**	**Small**	**Medium**
Tax	1.82***			1.52***		
	(0.24)			(0.23)		
Small	–0.13			0.39		
	(0.39)			(0.35)		
Medium	0.27	1.22**		0.92**	0.69	
	(0.43)	(0.60)		(0.40)	(0.55)	
Large	1.08**	1.76**	1.33	1.17***	0.90***	0.73
	(0.47)	(0.72)	(0.86)	(0.45)	(0.32)	(0.82)

(*Source*: Tchórzewska et al., 2022)

Note: We hereby report the average treatment effect on treated. The caliper is equal to 0.1. Standard errors are shown in parentheses. All standard errors are robust to firm heteroskedasticity. *** denotes significance at the 99% level, ** denotes significance at the 95% level, and * denotes significant at the 90% level.

capita as robustness. For each, firms facing different tax burdens are matched on observable pre-treatment characteristics, and average treatment effects are estimated across tax-intensity categories.

In the simplest treated-versus-untreated comparison, firms subject to environmental taxes invest substantially more in CP technologies than non-taxed firms. The estimated effect is large and statistically significant, indicating that, on average, taxing pollution is associated with a marked increase in process-integrated eco-innovation.

However, once the analysis differentiates between low, medium, and high tax payments, a more nuanced pattern emerges. Firms facing low or medium environmental tax levels—on the order of a few hundred to a few thousand euros per year—do not exhibit significantly higher cleaner production investment than comparable firms that pay no tax. In other words, low to modest tax burdens appear insufficient to shift behaviour meaningfully. It is only at the upper end of the tax distribution that a clear dose–response relationship becomes visible. Firms exposed to high environmental tax payments invest dramatically more in CP technologies than both non-taxed firms and those facing lower tax obligations. This suggests the presence of a threshold, below a certain level, environmental taxation is largely absorbed as a cost of doing business; beyond it, firms respond by undertaking more transformative, process-integrated upgrades.

Comparisons within the group of taxed firms further support this interpretation. Moving from lower to higher tax brackets is associated with additional increases in CP spending, consistent with a form of path dependence. Once firms have begun to adjust to environmental taxation, further strengthening of the price signal reinforces their commitment to cleaner technologies. Yet, the pattern is not strictly monotonic across every marginal step, indicating that adjustment may come in discrete investment episodes rather than as a smooth function of the tax rate.

The estimates for EP investments show a similar, though somewhat weaker structure. Environmental taxation is associated with higher spending on add-on abatement equipment, and medium to high tax levels in particular are linked to sizeable increases in EP investment. This is consistent with firms initially favouring relatively cheaper compliance options, such as filters or scrubbers, when the tax signal strengthens. At the same time, the absence of strong incremental effects between some adjacent tax categories hints that, once key EP investments are in place, additional tax increases may yield limited further response unless they are substantial enough to make a new round of upgrades worthwhile

Taken together, these findings deliver three important messages for the design of green fiscal policy. First, intensity matters. Symbolic or low-level environmental taxes on their own (without a comprehensive policy-mix) are unlikely to trigger significant green technology adoption. However, as we will show in Chapter 5, low levels of environmental taxation if combined with subsidies/tax credits can drive green technology adoption successfully. Second, there is evidence of non-linear responses and thresholds, particularly for CP technologies, which only respond strongly once taxation reaches higher levels. Third, environmental taxation appears capable of supporting both incremental (EP) and more structural (CP) adjustments, but the latter requires a stronger and more credible price signal. Thus, categorical treatment matching not only confirms that environmental taxes can work, but also helps identify the ranges in which they start to function as genuine drivers of eco-innovation rather than mere revenue instruments.

4.3.2 Regression discontinuity design

When the evaluative question is explicitly "at a threshold," RDD is often the cleanest route to causal inference, because it compares firms just below and just above a policy cut-off as to which should be nearly identical, except for the incentive they receive. In practice, however, RDD has been rarely (if at all) used for green fiscal instruments, largely because sharp eligibility rules are not always observable and firm-level data on green investment and adoption remain scarce. For that reason, it is useful to borrow a close analogue from Dechezleprêtre et al. (2023), who study UK R&D tax relief, where eligibility and generosity change discontinuously at firm-size thresholds.

Firms just below a threshold of total assets receive more generous R&D tax support than firms just above it. Dechezleprêtre et al. (2023) treat this cut-off as a quasi-experiment. If firms cannot perfectly manipulate their size to land on one side, then companies on either side of the threshold should be very similar in all respects, except for the generosity of the tax incentive. By comparing R&D spending and innovation outcomes (including quality-adjusted patents) immediately around the cut-off, they recover a local causal effect of receiving more generous tax relief.

Methodologically, this is a sharp RDD. The "running variable" is firm size, the "treatment" is enhanced tax relief, and the parameter of interest is the jump in innovation outcomes at the eligibility threshold. Because assignment is determined by an explicit rule, and because firms close to the cut-off are highly comparable, the resulting estimates are much closer to a causal effect than those from simple cross-sectional or fixed-effects regressions.

From the perspective of evaluating green fiscal policies, RDD offers several important advantages. Firstly and most importantly, RDD offers high internal validity. Because treatment is determined by a known rule at a cut-off, comparisons very close to the threshold mimic a randomised experiment. This is particularly valuable in policy settings where selection into support (e.g., applying for subsidies) is otherwise highly non-random. Secondly, it is amenable to rich outcomes. The same design can be applied not only to a broad range of eco-innovation outcomes but also to firm productivity measures.

At the same time, there are important limitations that policymakers and readers should keep in mind. Of course, RDD provides local but not global causal effects. RDD estimates the impact for firms close to the threshold. These local average treatment effects may not generalise to firms far from the cut-off (e.g., small firms or high polluters), thus external validity is limited. Secondly, the process of eligibility criteria must be clean, with no manipulations. The credibility of RDD rests on the assumption that firms cannot precisely sort around the cut-off based on unobserved factors correlated with outcomes. If firms bunch just below a threshold to secure generous green credits, or if reporting of the running variable (e.g., emissions, assets) is manipulable, estimates become biased. Density and balance tests are therefore essential. Additionally, reliable RDD requires micro-data (firm-level fiscal and innovation records merged from several sources) and enough of observations close to the threshold. In many countries, such data access is constrained, especially for environmental policy instruments at the firm level, even more so for green technology adoptions. Since this paper does not focus on green technology adoption, we shall not analyse the empirical results.

4.4 Can policy be redesigned to support energy efficiency and cleaner production?

Having established that green fiscal instruments can be effective on average, proportional increase leads to increase in green technology adoption and having established the minimum "dose" of the policy instrument. The final question is whether policy can be redesigned to steer firms towards the technologies we consider superior—namely, energy-efficiency improvements and cleaner production, rather than incremental EP fixes.

In this section, I answer this question by drawing on two complementary strands of evidence. Tchorzewska (2024) uses a DiD design around tax-credit reform to show how redesigning a single instrument can shift firm investment towards CP technologies, while Yamazaki (2017) shows how environmental taxation can be paired with tax revenue recycling—to ease competitiveness concerns while reinforcing incentives for energy efficiency.

4.4.1 Difference-in-difference

In the previous sections, we examined how a DiD strategy combined with IVs can be used to assess the effectiveness of introducing a carbon tax in a British context. By construction, DiD designs are particularly well suited to analyse changes in existing policy instruments, as illustrated in the recent application by Tchorzewska (2024) to reforms of the Environmental Investment (EI) tax credit.

The author uses the reform of the Spanish EI tax credit in 2011, which offered a useful quasi-natural experiment for assessing how stricter and more targeted rules shape firms' green investment decisions. After a gradual phase-out of the original, relatively generous, and undifferentiated tax credit, the government unexpectedly reintroduced the EI credit in March 2011, with more demanding conditions towards CP technologies. In other words, it made it more difficult to finance inferior EP technologies, which were already majorly obligatory through environmental regulations, with this particular tax incentive. This abrupt policy reversal, combined with firm-level panel data, creates a setting well suited to a DiD strategy (Figure 4.1).

The core idea is to compare how investment in green technologies evolves over time for firms that make use of the reintroduced EI tax credit (the *treated* group) relative to firms that do not claim it (the *control* group), before and after 2011. In practice, the empirical model relates the log of firm-level green investment—distinguishing between CP and EP technologies—to an interaction between (i) an indicator for claiming the EI tax credit and (ii) a post-2011 time dummy. Firm fixed effects absorb all time-invariant differences between users and non-users of the credit (such as underlying environmental orientation, management quality, or technological capacity), while year fixed effects capture macroeconomic shocks, the financial crisis, and other policy changes common to all firms. Additional controls include firm size and lagged green investment, and standard errors are clustered at the firm level to account for serial correlation. The model specification, thus, looks as follows in specification (4.4):

$$\begin{aligned} \ln\_invest_{it} = {} & \beta_0 + \beta_1 dtaxcred_{it} + \beta_2 dpost2011_{it} \\ & + \delta\left(taxcred * post2011\right)_{it} + \theta X_{it} + \alpha_i + \alpha_t + \epsilon_{it} \end{aligned} \tag{4.4}$$

In this setup, the coefficient on the interaction term delta (δ), the DiD estimator, measures the average percentage change in green technology adoption associated with access to the more stringent EI tax credit after 2011, over and above general time trends and stable firm characteristics. The logic is that, if treated and control firms followed similar trajectories before the reform (the parallel trends assumption), any systematic divergence thereafter can be attributed, at least in part, to the changed tax credit rules.

To explore dynamics and heterogeneity, the baseline specification is extended in two directions. First, an event-study style model replaces the single post-2011 dummy with a series of year-by-year interactions, tracing how the effect builds up or fades out over time in specification (4.5). Second, a triple-differences specification interacts treatment with the post-reform period and size-group indicators to examine whether responses differ between smaller and larger firms in specification (4.6). The model specifications look as follows:

$$\ln\_invest_{it} = \sum_{T=0}^{m} \gamma_T \left(dtaxcred * year\right)_{it} + \rho_1 taxcred_{it} + \theta X_{it} + \alpha_i + \alpha_t + \epsilon_{it} \tag{4.5}$$

$$\ln\_invest_{it} = \sigma(dtaxcred * dpost2011 * sizegr)_{it} + dtaxcred_{it} + \theta X_{it} + \alpha_i + \alpha_t + \epsilon_{it} \tag{4.6}$$

In equation (4.5), the model includes interaction terms between the tax-credit dummy ($d\_taxcredit$) and separate year dummies, alongside standard time and firm fixed effects and a full set of control variables. In equation (4.6), the specification instead interacts the tax-credit dummy ($d\_taxcredit$) with the policy-change dummy ($d\_post2011$) and the heterogeneous group indicator of interest ($sizegr$). Again, all standard firm-level controls are included, together with year and firm fixed effects. In both specifications, standard errors are clustered at the firm level.

This strategy has several advantages for evaluating modifications in existing tax credits. It directly exploits an unexpected policy change, which happened in 2011, thus reducing concerns that firms may have timed their investments in anticipation. By combining DiD with firm fixed effects, it also absorbs many sources of selection on levels, for example, that firms inclined to invest in environmental technologies are also more likely to learn about and claim tax credits. The event-study extension provides a visual and statistical check of pre-trends, which strengthens the credibility of the identification strategy. Moreover, the design remains relatively transparent. Policymakers can clearly see how, conditional on observables and fixed effects, treated and control firms diverge once the new rules come into force. We can thus see that DiD strategy provides estimates that have both relatively high internal and external validities.

There are, however, important limitations. The absence of strict eligibility criteria means that self-selection into treatment is not fully exogenous. Firms that claim the credit are precisely those that invest in eligible technologies and are informed about the instrument, which may reflect unobserved differences in capabilities, expectations, or strategic orientation. If these factors also shape trends in green investment, the DiD estimates may still be biased, even with fixed effects. The approach further relies on the parallel trends' assumption, which, although partially testable using pre-2011 dynamics, can never be definitively verified. In addition, the estimated effects are average responses for users versus non-users and may conceal substantial heterogeneity. For instance, stronger impacts among credit-constrained firms or technology leaders. Finally, overlapping policy changes or sector-specific shocks

Table 4.5 The main difference-in-difference results from making the EI tax credit more demanding towards cleaner-production technologies

	(1) *lnEPair*	(2) *lnCPair*	(3) *lnCPenc*
post2011	0.0173	0.343*	−0.0475
	(0.157)	(0.189)	(0.181)
dtaxcred	5.302***	7.501***	2.384***
	(0.813)	(0.876)	(0.720)
diff	−1.674*	−0.0930	1.249
	(0.946)	(1.129)	(0.895)
Observations	11,487	11,487	11,487
R-squared	0.046	0.067	0.038

(*Source*: Tchorzewska, 2024)

Note: Each coefficient is estimated from different regression following the main specification. The dependent variables are the amount in the log of equipment investment. This measure is used for several types of technologies. Acronyms CP and EP denote investments into cleaner production and end-of-pipe technologies, respectively. Ending air denotes investments specifically for air pollution reduction, while ending enc denotes reduction of energy consumption. Additional controls include firm size, lagged investment, firm, and year fixed effects. Standard errors in parentheses are clustered at the firm level. ***$p < 0.01$, **$p < 0.05$, and *$p < 0.1$.

around 2011 may contaminate the estimated treatment effect if they are not adequately controlled for. Randomised control experiments would solve all those problems.

With regards to useful policy implications, the results reported in this framework generally indicate that the reintroduction of the EI tax credit with tighter rules is associated with a statistically and economically meaningful decline in investment in the inferior EP technologies, which makes this EI tax-credit modification a conservative success. Those results are especially visible in Table 4.5, where we can observe negative and statistically significant coefficient on filters and sulphur scrubbers (model specification 1, lnEPair). While the coefficient for energy-efficient technologies (model specification 3, lnCPenc) is not statistically significant, it is positive, suggesting that some firms did use this sudden reintroduction of a green tax incentive to invest in superior green technologies. Indeed, Figure 4.3 shows the heterogeneity analyses with respect to firm size, and we can observe that tax credits typically show positive and large effects for smallest firms (below 50 employees), for whom tax relief more strongly relaxes financial constraints; while for the biggest firms (above 200 employees), we can see the reverse.

These findings carry several policy implications. First, they support the view that well-designed, more selective tax credits can deliver genuine additionality in eco-innovation, rather than simply subsidising investments

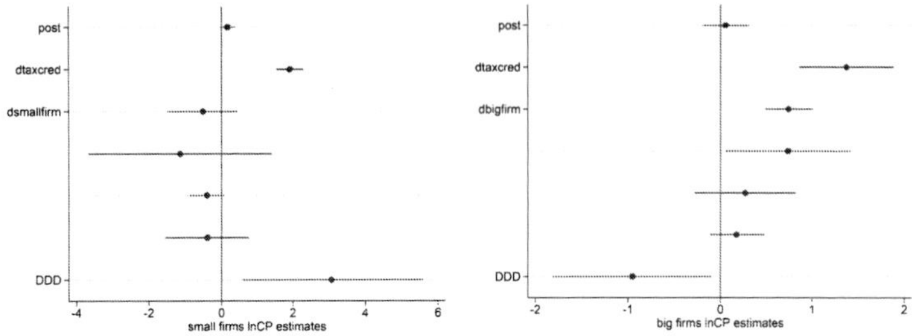

Figure 4.3 Heterogeneous effects on cleaner production technologies (lnCP) with respect to different firm sizes

(*Source*: Tchorzewska, 2024)

that would have occurred anyway. Second, they highlight the importance of clarity and credibility. An unexpectedly reintroduced, rules-based credit still induced a measurable response, suggesting that stable and predictable frameworks might be even more effective. Third, the stronger impact on CP investments points to the potential of targeted tax incentives to steer the composition of green investment away from marginal EP fixes and towards more transformative process changes. Fourth, the years that this study used were 2008–2014, thus the years of the financial crises. The following study shows that the properly designed tax credit can induce higher investment into CP technologies for the smallest firms even during the recession times. Finally, the methodological lesson is forward-looking, designing green tax-credit schemes around clear, verifiable criteria, and documenting changes precisely, creates the conditions under which DiD and related quasi-experimental tools can be used to rigorously evaluate and refine policy over time. This strategy will also prove useful in the evaluation of green fiscal policy phase-out—as we will show in Chapter 6 in detail, albeit, with significant improvements.

Finally, we can see that this section answered the last research question and showed that green fiscal policies can be modified successfully, as to discourage pollution-abating technologies, and incentivise CP technologies, especially for smallest businesses.

4.4.2 Difference-in-difference with environmental tax revenue recycling

Having introduced the DiD approach, I now would like to illustrate a useful extension drawing on Yamazaki (2017), which evaluates British Columbia's revenue-neutral carbon tax using an industry-level DiD that compares outcomes in the province with those in the rest of Canada. For present purposes, the value of the study lies less in its outcome focus—employment rather than green technology adoption—than in its modelling architecture, which renders the policy's design features, especially revenue recycling, analytically transparent. For this reason, I will limit myself to the explanation of the introduction of tax revenue into the specification model.

The specification links the rising carbon tax to pre-existing industry characteristics such as emissions intensity and trade exposure to trace the cost-side channels through which higher energy prices affect employment, while simultaneously incorporating revenue recycling by constructing a revenue proxy from baseline emissions interacted with the tax rate. With industry-by-year fixed effects absorbing common shocks and industry-by-province fixed effects capturing time-invariant structural differences, the remaining variation identifies how more emissions-intensive or more trade-exposed industries in British Columbia evolve relative to comparable industries elsewhere as the tax increases—and, crucially, whether the recycling of revenues through cuts in personal and corporate income taxes offsets those cost pressures.

The estimates indicate that the redistribution channel is positive for employment, implying that returning carbon revenues via reductions in distortionary taxes can mitigate or even counterbalance adverse labour-market effects. We can observe that credible, revenue-neutral design can widen the political and economic room for stronger price signals, thereby making it more feasible to sustain the kinds of carbon prices that, in principle, also encourage cleaner production and energy efficiency.

4.5 Conclusions

This chapter has examined how modern empirical methods are used to evaluate individual green fiscal policy instruments, with a focus on three core dimensions: effectiveness (do they work?), dose–response/intensity (how strong must they be?), and design and redesign (can they be successfully redesigned?). Taken together, the evidence provides a coherent set of lessons on what tends to work, under what conditions, and how we know it.

Firstly, we have answered the four research questions. We now know that green fiscal policy instruments can be effective, especially at driving energy-efficient technologies, but only if they are designed correctly. We have also seen that green fiscal policy instruments tend to have proportional effects, especially on process-integrated technologies; and that average levels may mask substantial heterogeneity across tax levels. Low levels of green fiscal policy instruments are typically not effective at driving energy-efficient technologies. Lastly, we have shown that existing green fiscal policy instruments can be modified such that they finance more CP technologies, rather than EP technologies.

Regarding the conclusions coming from the methods. Across this literature, simple fixed-effects models are a useful starting point. They allow a comparison of several policy tools within a consistent framework and help detect broad patterns. However, as stressed throughout the chapter, fixed effects alone are rarely sufficient for causal claims, given targeted policy design and selection into treatment.

A second message concerns the dose–response properties of green fiscal instruments. Here, categorical treatment matching, continuous dose–response approaches, and designs exploiting variation in tax or support intensity converge on a clear conclusion—marginal, symbolic interventions tend to do little. For environmental taxes, low and unstable rates are often absorbed as routine costs and fail to shift firms' behaviour. Only beyond certain thresholds do we observe substantial increases in investment in both end-of-pipe and, more importantly, CP technologies. Similarly, for subsidies and tax credits, very small incentives are ineffective, while excessively generous schemes risk funding inframarginal projects and inflating fiscal costs. Methodologically, categorical treatment matching is particularly valuable in highlighting this non-linearity and should be applied only in suitable institutional settings. By comparing firms facing different tax or support "doses," it reveals where incentives start to bite and where they simply recycle resources without additional eco-innovation.

A third methodological lesson concerns threshold-based evaluation, where RDD often provides the cleanest causal leverage. As Dechezleprêtre et al. (2023) illustrate, when support generosity changes discretely at a clear eligibility rule—such as a firm-size cut-off—firms just below and just above the threshold are otherwise highly comparable, so the discontinuity yields estimates close to experimental evidence. While their application is to general R&D and patents, the same identification logic applies to eco-innovation tax credits whenever green schemes are structured around sharp size, emissions, or expenditure thresholds that generate quasi-experiments. The main caveat is that RDD delivers high-internal validity, but inherently local, average treatment effects that should not be extrapolated beyond firms near the cut-off or to different policy levels.

Lastly, to study introductions, policy modifications, and other exogenous shocks, one can combine fixed-effects models with difference-in-difference analysis. Here, the granularity of data combined with the appropriate institutional setting leads to results high in internal and external validity. Thus, such studies as Tchorzewska (2024) and Yamazaki (2017) become the best source of data on how the green fiscal policies perform in reality, and hence, the empirical methods and policy design are most visibly intertwined. The DiD evidence from Tchorzewska (2024) indicates that tightening eligibility towards cleaner production can shift the *composition* of investment away from inferior EP technologies and, in particular for smaller firms, relax financial constraints in ways that support more transformative energy-efficient process upgrades. Finally, Yamazaki's (2017) analysis of British Columbia's revenue-neutral carbon tax shows that the use of revenues holds high potential. Recycling carbon receipts through cuts in labour and capital taxes can offset the employment costs of higher energy prices, making strong price signals more politically and economically sustainable.

Overall, the lesson that emerges is that there is no single "best" green fiscal instrument, but there are better and worse ways of designing them. Instruments need to be strong enough to move behaviour, calibrated so that public resources finance genuinely additional investments, and structured so that eligibility rules can be used. Revenue recycling can be an interesting additional to green fiscal policies. Subsequent chapters will build on these insights by examining how to evaluate policy-mixes and how firms react to a green fiscal policy phase-out.

5 Modern empirical evaluations of environmental policy-mixes

5.1 Introduction

Firms almost never face environmental instruments in isolation (OECD, 2025b); in fact, some researchers claim that we live in times of policy-mess rather than a well-coordinated policy-mix (Greco et al., 2022). Whereas Chapter 4 examined modern methods for estimating effects of individual policy tools, most real-world decisions about process eco-innovation occur under *simultaneous exposure* to multiple instruments; at a single moment in time or over a longer period. This chapter therefore shifts the unit of analysis from single policies to policy-mixes and develops empirical strategies to identify their interaction effects, sequencing, and credibility.

From a welfare perspective, mixes can be (i) complements that lower multiple margins of frictions (cost, risk, learning), (ii) substitutes that crowd out private effort or other instruments, or (iii) conflicting when design features blunt incentives or shift them intertemporally, and (iv) independent (Carree et al., 2011; Mohnen and Roller, 2005). Empirically, the relevant question is which combinations and sequences are effective in incentivising cleaner-production (CP) technologies.

Building on Chapter 4's single-policy estimators, this chapter assembles a toolkit for existing multi-treatment causal inference in environmental economics. It provides operational guidance on (i) identifying interaction at a single point in time and (ii) sequencing effects and answers the following research questions. Do the green fiscal policy instruments, for example, environmental taxes, subsidies, and tax credits seem to be complements, substitutes, or independent? What are the doses at which policy-mixes between environmental taxation and public financing are most effective? Does the ordering of green fiscal policy instruments matter for green technology adoption?

5.2 How can we analyse static green fiscal policy-mixes?

In this chapter, I use the term static policy-mix to refer to the configuration of green fiscal instruments at a given point in time, abstracting from how these instruments may evolve or be phased-in and -out over the years. The focus is

DOI: 10.4324/9781003712398-5

thus on how different taxes, subsidies, tax credits coexist and interact within a single year, and on how this configuration shapes firms' behaviour—green technology adoption. I introduce and compare several methodological strategies for evaluating such static policy-mixes and architectures.

5.2.1 Fixed-effects model with interaction effects

A large empirical literature examines what drives firms to adopt cleaner process-integrated production technologies and improve energy efficiency (del Río et al., 2016, Horbach et al., 2012; Lilliestam et al., 2021; Jaffe & Palmer, 1997; Jaffe et al., 2002; Kerr & Newell, 2003; Requate, 1995). These studies typically evaluate *drivers* of eco-innovation and often distinguish between cleaner-production (CP) and end-of-pipe (EP) investments (Demirel & Kesidou, 2011; Frondel et al., 2007, Horbach, 2008; Rennings, 2000).

Building on that tradition, a natural way to move from single instruments to policy-mixes is to estimate a panel model with firm and year fixed effects and explicit interaction terms among policy variables and to also include organisational capabilities. Consider an extension of the specification used in García-Quevedo et al. (2022), which allows for interactions among environmental taxes, green investment subsidies, and environmental investment tax credits (equation 5.1):

$$\begin{aligned}\ln\left(\text{ECOIN}_{it}\right) = {} & \rho \ln\left(\text{ECOIN}_{i,t-1}\right) + \beta_1\, D\text{Taxes}_{it} + \beta_2\, D\text{Subsidies}_{it} \\ & + \beta_3\, D\text{TaxCredits}_{it} + \beta_{12}\left(D\text{Taxes}_{it} \times D\text{Subsidies}_{it}\right) \\ & + \beta_{13}\left(D\text{Taxes}_{it} \times D\text{TaxCredits}_{it}\right) \\ & + \beta_{23}\left(D\text{Subsidies}_{it} \times D\text{TaxCredits}_{it}\right) \\ & + \beta_{123}\left(D\text{Taxes}_{it} \times D\text{Subsidies}_{it} \times D\text{TaxCredits}_{it}\right) \\ & + \theta_1\, D\text{GreenEmp}_{it} + \theta_2\, D\text{EnvCert}_{it} + \gamma' \mathbf{X}_{it} \\ & + \alpha_i + \alpha_s + \tau_t + \varepsilon_{it}.\end{aligned} \tag{5.1}$$

Here, $\ln\left(ECOIN_{it}\right)$ is firm i's log expenditure on eco-innovation in year t (either CP or EP technologies). The lagged dependent variable $\ln\left(ECOIN_{i,t-1}\right)$ captures path dependence. $DTaxes_{it}$, $DSubsidies_{it}$, and $DTaxCredits_{it}$ indicate exposure to, or uptake of, the respective instruments, as we included them in Chapter 4. However, this time, we extend the model by the inclusion of the pairwise interaction terms ($\beta_{12}, \beta_{13}, \beta_{23}$), which identify whether instruments are complements (> 0) or substitutes (< 0) when used jointly, and the triple interaction term β_{123}, which captures the higher-order mix effects. $DGreenEmp_{it}$ and $DEnvCert_{it}$ proxy organisational capabilities; X_it includes standard controls (e.g., size). Firm fixed effects (α_i) absorb time-invariant heterogeneity (managerial quality, culture, baseline technology), sector firm effects (α_s) capture environmental regulations at the sectoral level, constant across time and year fixed effects (τ_t) capture aggregate shocks (macroeconomy, national policy shifts, energy prices).

Just as in the case of evaluating individual fiscal policies, models with fixed effects and interaction terms offer a direct, yet, rather crude test of policy complementarities. Interaction coefficients quantify whether instruments amplify or blunt each other. Additionally, the method is flexible and transparent. The design accommodates different uptake intensities and organisational moderators (green staff, certifications, and other firm-level time-invariant characteristics) while remaining easy to communicate.

This strategy has several weaknesses that call for cautious interpretation. Extensive interaction terms can create limited-support problems when some policy bundles are rare, so "complementarities" are identified from a narrow subset of observations and rely on extrapolation; multicollinearity further inflates standard errors and makes results sensitive to small specification changes. With many interactions in two-way fixed-effects models, non-standard group–time weighting (including negative weights) can render coefficients hard to interpret, effectively averaging heterogeneous effects rather than isolating a clean bundle contrast. The setup is also static, pushing anticipation, adjustment dynamics, and policy lags into the error term and risking bias if these dynamics differ across mixes. Finally, policy bundles are often endogenously adopted by more capable or influential jurisdictions, and fixed effects address only time-invariant selection, so without stronger identification the interaction estimates are best read as correlations rather than causal effects. Hence, exactly as in evaluations of individual instruments, one must keep in mind endogenous policy timing and uptake. Adoption of an environmental tax, subsidy, or tax credit—and firms' decisions to take it up—may respond to unobserved, time-varying shocks such as impending modernisation, lobbying cycles, or local political bargains. This makes it all the more important to complement fixed-effects interaction models with additional quasi-experimental structure. We will analyse those in more detail in the forthcoming sections of Chapter 5.

Table 5.1 reports fixed-effects estimates with interaction terms (eq. 5.1) and suggests a nuanced pattern in the static policy-mix, which as we mentioned should be taken with caution. In the preferred specifications, investment subsidies are consistently associated with higher spending on both CP and EP technologies, even after controlling for the wider instrument set. Tax credits, by contrast, remain primarily linked to CP investment rather than to that of EP, consistent with the baseline results. The interaction capturing the joint presence of an environmental tax and an investment subsidy indicates

Table 5.1 Main results: Fixed-effects regression estimations for log investment in CP and EP using interaction terms for policy-mixes

	lnCP (1)	*lnEP* (2)
L.1	−0.04***	−0.05***
	(0.01)	(0.01)
dtax	0.28	0.06
	(0.29)	(0.28)
dsub	1.35**	1.18**
	(0.55)	(0.48)
dtcred	4.22***	0.14
	(0.74)	(0.69)
dtax # dtcred	−1.07	1.60
	(1.13)	(1.08)
dtax # dsub	2.16*	−0.70
	(1.12)	(1.10)
dtcred # dsub	0.01	0.80
	(1.28)	(1.37)
dtax # dsub # dtcred	−5.10***	2.16
	(2.28)	(2.67)
dgreen_empl	1.04***	1.36***
	(0.36)	(0.35)
denv_cert	0.63**	0.00
	(0.32)	(0.29)
size dummies	×	×
time FE	×	×
firm FE	×	×
N	14,528	14,528
F stat	9.65	21.92
Prob >F	0.00	0.00

(*Source*: García-Quevedo et al., 2022)

Note: All standard errors are clustered at the firm level. ***, **, and * denote significance at the 99% level, 95% level, and 90% level, respectively. Mean Variance Inflation Factor (VIF) is equal to 8.18.

a modestly estimated, potentially reinforcing effect on CP investment, but not EP (which is in agreement with the theory presented in Chapter 3). By comparison, the triple interaction of tax, subsidy, and tax credit is negative and sizeable, implying that dense policy layering may become counterproductive—through overlapping incentives, informational burden, or crowding-out. For EP investment, subsidies are the only instrument with a stable, statistically robust positive association, reinforcing the view that firms rely on them as the main financing lever for pollution-abatement projects unless schemes are designed to avoid this. Overall, the results point to subsidies as a broad and powerful instrument, tax credits as more process-oriented, and heavy stacking of tools as potentially risky without coordination—though the richest bundles are observed for relatively few units, so the corresponding interaction estimates rest on thin support and should be read cautiously.

Thus, we are addressing the first research question of this chapter, showing that environmental taxes and public financing, for example, subsidies or tax credits can be positively correlated with green technology adoption under the right policy design; however, they can also be negatively correlated if too many policy tools are offered at once.

5.2.2 Complementarity analysis

The preceding section used fixed effects with interaction terms to explore whether pairs or triplets of instruments appear to correlate with green technology adoption. This is a natural first step, interactions reveal whether the association between one policy and the outcome varies systematically with the presence or intensity of another. Yet, without additional structure, such estimates remain, at best, strong correlations. A more demanding notion—better aligned with what a policy-mix chapter typically seeks—is complementarity analysis (Resende et al., 2014). Rather than asking whether the coefficient on $A \times B$ is positive, it tests whether policy inputs are supermodular in the outcome. Whether strengthening one instrument increases the marginal effectiveness of another, that is, whether the mix produces more than the sum of its parts.

This approach is rooted in the innovation-policy literature. Mohnen and Röller (2005) developed complementarity tests for binary inputs (adopt/not adopt), and Carree et al. (2011) extended the framework to continuous inputs and multiple practices. Despite its conceptual fit for environmental policy-mixes, firm-level applications to green fiscal instruments and green technology adoption remain, to our knowledge, absent—largely for practical reasons. Thus, the research question of green fiscal policies being complements or substitutes was not fully tested. Formal complementarity tests require rich, simultaneous micro-level variation and well-measured intensities across several instruments, conditions that are rarely satisfied in administrative environmental policy data.

Recent eco-innovation work nonetheless illustrates both the promise and the empirical demands of the method (Ayoub and Lhuillery, 2024; Garcia-Piqueres & Garcia-Ramos, 2024; Mazzanti & Zoboli, 2008; Ozusaglam et al., 2018). Ayoub and Lhuillery (2024), for example, analyse 5,416 innovating firms in France (2008–2014) and test whether green Research & Development (R&D), biotech R&D, and Information and Communication Technology (ICT) R&D are complements in generating eco-product and eco-process innovation. Their strategy first models the two innovation outcomes jointly with a bivariate probit with sample selection, allowing correlated unobservables, and then implements complementarity tests for continuous inputs following Carree et al. (2011). In doing so, they estimate effects of the three intensities alongside all pairwise and triple interactions, and then re-parameterise the model so that supermodularity translates into sign restrictions on specific linear combinations of coefficients—requirements that are stricter than simply finding a positive interaction term, because they demand consistency across multiple margins, including the higher-order interaction.

As we have mentioned above, the workable empirical strategy begins with a panel specification with firm fixed effects, including levels and interactions for each policy, along with standard controls for size, sector–year shocks, input prices, and lagged outcomes. The next step is to re-organise the parameterisation à la Carree et al. (2011), such that complementarity becomes a set of testable sign restrictions. For example:

$$\alpha_{12} \geq 0 \ \textit{and} \ \alpha_{12} + \alpha_{123} \geq 0 \tag{5.2}$$

with at least one holding strictly. In case of the study by Ayoub and Lhuillery (2024), the model investigates:

$$Y_i = \alpha_1 x_1 + \alpha_2 x_2 + \alpha_3 x_3 + \alpha_{\{12\}} x_1 x_2 + \alpha_{\{13\}} x_1 x_3 + \alpha_{\{23\}} x_2 x_3 + \alpha_{\{123\}} x_1 x_2 x_3 + \varepsilon_i \tag{5.3}$$

which is consequently modified into:

$$\begin{aligned} Y_i = {} & \alpha_1 x_1 + \alpha_2 x_2 + \alpha_3 x_3 + \alpha_{\{12\}} \left(x_1 x_2 - x_1 x_2 x_3 \right) + \alpha_{\{13\}} x_1 x_3 + \alpha_{\{23\}} x_2 x_3 \\ & + \left(\alpha_{\{12\}} + \alpha_{\{123\}} \right) x_1 x_2 x_3 + \varepsilon_i \end{aligned} \tag{5.4}$$

To assess whether any two inputs act as complements in the presence of a third, the authors re-parameterise the model in the way shown above (equations 5.3 and 5.4) such that the key objects are (i) the coefficient on $x_1 x_2 - x_1 x_2 x_3$, which equals α_{12}, and (ii) the coefficient on $x_1 x_2 x_3$, which equals $\alpha_{12} + \alpha_{123}$. Complementarity between x_1 and x_2 (conditional on x_3) requires both weak supermodularity inequalities, $\alpha_{12} \geq 0$ and $\alpha_{12} + \alpha_{123} \geq 0$, with at least one holding strictly. Empirically, they inspect the t-statistics for these two linear combinations, call them t_1 (for α_{12}) and t_2 (for $\alpha_{12} + \alpha_{123}$), and reject the null of no complementarity if the inequalities are satisfied and the estimates show statistical support such that either $t_1 > t_c$ and $t_2 > t_d$ or $t_1 > t_d$ and $t_2 > t_c$, where the critical values are $t_c = 1.96$ and $t_d = 1.65$ (two-sided).

Complementarity analysis offers a more precise way to study policy-mix synergies and conflicts. Rather than inferring complementarity from a single positive interaction term, it tests a clearly defined property—supermodularity—of the outcome function in policy instruments. If instruments A and B are complements in this sense, then raising A increases the marginal payoff to B. The framework also scales beyond two instruments, allowing the researcher to examine whether a third tool amplifies or attenuates a pairwise relationship.

These strengths come with important limitations that should temper interpretation. First, the approach is data-intensive. It requires well-measured, continuous firm-level intensities for multiple instruments and sufficient joint variation across those instruments. Many environmental policies are binary or observed only in aggregate, so firm-level exposure must often be imputed, inviting measurement error that can bias tests of supermodularity towards null findings. Second, identification remains challenging. Environmental instruments are frequently targeted to sectors, regions, or firms already on greener trajectories, and multiple instruments often move together for the same units. Without plausibly exogenous timing, supermodularity tests risk validating persistent selection or simultaneity rather than genuine complementarities. Third, the tests are functional-form dependent. Supermodularity is assessed within a chosen parameterisation of the outcome function; misspecification can generate false positives or negatives. Relatedly, inference becomes fragile when the joint distribution of policy intensities has thin support—for example, very few observations with both high tax and high subsidy—or when instruments are highly collinear. Fourth, statistical power can be limited. Because the null involves multiple inequalities (including pairwise and conditional complementarities), rejecting non-complementarity typically requires tighter estimates than in a simple interaction-test framework, which is demanding in short panels, with rare outcomes, or under noisy exposure measures. Fifth, dynamics and interference complicate interpretation. Complementarities may be intertemporal or spatial, stretching standard panel and Stable Unit Treatment Value Assumption (SUTVA) assumptions. Thus, complementarity analysis is therefore best viewed as a gold-standard robustness check that sits on top of fixed-effects models with interaction terms.

5.2.3 Categorical treatment matching

A useful way to investigate green fiscal policy-mixes more seriously, without imposing linearity or functional-form restrictions, is to use categorical treatment matching. Rather than treating "policy" as a single binary switch, firms are classified into mutually exclusive treatment categories, and outcomes are compared across units that look similar ex ante but face different bundles and intensities of instruments. Within this framework, it becomes possible to contrast firms exposed to two instruments (e.g., an environmental tax plus public financing) with comparable firms exposed to only one ("tax only" or "subsidy only"), and to do so in a way that respects both heterogeneity in dose and the fact that real-world instruments arrive in bundles.

Implementation proceeds in two main steps. The first is to define policy relevant categories that capture discrete regimes rather than a single continuous treatment. Following Tchórzewska et al. (2022), as discussed in Chapter 4, environmental taxation can be divided into terciles of the firm-level distribution, low, medium, and high, augmented by an untreated group comprising firms with no environmental tax payment. This yields four mutually exclusive tax categories (0, 1, 2, 3). Public aid, in the form of subsidies and/or tax credits, can then be layered as a second dimension, generating a set of policy-mix cells such as "tax–low + aid" or "tax–medium + aid." In this way, the multi-category setup preserves heterogeneity in tax intensity while making explicit comparisons such as "tax–medium + aid" versus "tax–medium only" possible, which a single continuous dose–response curve would struggle to represent as transparently.

The second step is to match firms across these categories on the basis of their pre-treatment characteristics, as we showed in the earlier chapter. This is typically done by estimating category-specific propensity scores—e.g., through a system of binary logits—using covariates such as firm size, sector, balance-sheet indicators, pre-trends in investment, etc. Firms are then matched across categories on their estimated scores, using a caliper to ensure closeness of matches and standard diagnostics to verify common support. Treatment effects are recovered as pairwise contrasts among matched firms, for instance, comparing two instruments versus tax only, two instruments versus aid only, and each instrument alone versus no policy. Where data permit, finer partitions can be explored as robustness checks, but there is an inevitable trade-off between granularity and the thickness of common support.

The credibility of categorical treatment matching rests on the key identifying assumption—unconfoundedness, as we have stated in Chapter 4. That is conditional on observed covariates, assignment to treatment categories must be independent of potential outcomes. If programme managers systematically steer firms into aid programmes or into higher-intensity policy mixes on the basis of unobserved traits—managerial quality or technological readiness—then estimated treatment effects will be biased. Common support is a second pressure point. The method requires sufficient overlap in the distribution of propensity scores across categories; when the two-instrument regime is rare, finding credible matches becomes difficult. Trimming observations with weak support can improve internal validity, but at the cost of statistical power and external generalisability.

A further limitation is that the basic design is essentially static. Categorical matching identifies differences across regimes at a given time, but it does not, on its own, identify policy sequence. It cannot distinguish aid-then-tax from tax-then-aid nor can it easily capture dynamic responses unless the categories themselves are redefined over rolling windows. The measurement of exposure also matters. If tax intensity is mismeasured—for example, if accruals, refunds, or offsets are not properly captured—or if aid is recorded as commitments rather than disbursements, estimates will tend to be attenuated towards zero. The more continuous, timely, and economically meaningful the exposure measures, the more informative and interpretable the matches.

Table 5.2 Comparison of the effectiveness of public aid, environmental taxes alone as well as a policy-mix (outcome variables: lnCP and lnEP)

	Just environmental tax		*Just public aid*		*Both vs. none*		*Both vs. public aid*	
	lnCP	**lnEP**	**lnCP**	**lnEP**	**lnCP**	**lnEP**	**lnCP**	**lnEP**
Tax	1.82*** (0.24)	1.52*** (0.23)	5.09*** (0.51)	3.57*** (0.50)	5.90*** (0.78)	5.19*** (0.83)	2.50** (1.06)	1.61~ (0.98)
Small	−0.13 (0.39)	0.39 (0.35)	3.54** (0.89)	2.43** (0.92)	4.95*** (1.49)	5.21*** (1.41)	−0.36 (1.50)	−0.67 (1.57)
Medium	0.27 (0.43)	0.92** (0.40)	7.61*** (0.92)	4.51*** (0.85)	8.51*** (1.45)	8.20*** (1.31)	−0.34 (1.50)	0.85 (1.57)
Large	1.08** (0.47)	1.17*** (0.45)	7.93*** (0.88)	5.99*** (0.85)	4.44** (1.46)	2.67 (1.70)	2.26* (1.62)	4.43*** (1.73)

(*Source*: Tchórzewska et al., 2022)

Note: Average treatment effect on treated. Caliper = 0.1. Standard errors in parentheses; heteroskedasticity-robust. ***, **, and * *denote 1%, 5%, and 10% significance;* ~ denotes almost 10% significance. *Obs: 1,983 (tax only), 499 (public financing only), 213 (both), and 8,878 (none)*

Within these constraints, several design choices can substantially improve credibility. The encoding of exposure should be economically meaningful. Constructing tax terciles relative to an appropriate base (per unit of energy use, per unit of value added, or per employee) yields categories that map more closely onto underlying cost signals. Similarly, aid is best measured as an effective stimulus—such as the present value of support relative to eligible capital expenditure—rather than as a mere binary. Considerable effort should be invested in balance and overlap diagnostics. Reporting standardised differences before and after matching, presenting common-support plots, and examining the sensitivity of results to different calipers or alternative balancing schemes (such as entropy balancing or inverse-probability weighting) are essential steps (Table 5.2).

The empirical results, presented in Table 5.3, show estimates of treatment effects for CP and EP investments under different policy regimes. Public aid, for example, grants or tax credits tied to green capital expenditure appears as the single most reliable driver of CP investment and, to a lesser extent, EP equipment. Relative to a "no-policy" counterfactual, aid alone yields large, precise gains across firm sizes. This is exactly what a finance-frictions perspective would predict. CP projects with measurable energy savings are constrained by first costs; when liquidity arrives and investment risk is partially eliminated, projects start.

Environmental taxation on its own exhibits positive but smaller and more heterogeneous effects. Its impact is most evident on EP investment,

Table 5.3 Results of a sequential analysis—Fixed-effects regression estimates for averages of log investment into adoption of green technologies and environmental R&D over a five-year window using sequencing strategy. Columns report coefficients with standard errors in parentheses

	avglnCP (1)	*avglnCPair* (2)	*avglnCPenc* (3)	*avglnEP* (4)	*avglnEPair* (5)	*avgllnRD* (6)
Sequence						
Order envtax, taxcred	0.76 (0.57)	0.25 (0.49)	0.36 (0.91)	0.65 (0.98)	0.22 (0.59)	0.41 (0.33)
Order envtax, sub	1.49 (0.77)	0.58* (0.34)	0.95* (0.49)	0.54 (0.89)	0.25 (0.63)	−0.19 (0.29)
Order taxcred, envtax	1.47 (0.99)	0.24 (0.42)	0.45 (0.54)	0.42 (0.81)	0.20 (0.62)	0.07 (0.36)
Order taxcred, sub	−1.42 (0.70)	−1.60*** (0.46)	−2.06* (1.05)	3.15 (1.46)	1.40 (0.76)	0.26 (0.29)
Order sub, envtax	0.19 (0.59)	0.29 (0.91)	0.78 (0.79)	6.67 (6.07)	0.75 (0.27)	0.48 (0.48)
Order sub, taxcred	−1.70 (0.57)	−2.96** (0.89)	−2.49* (1.27)	1.87 (1.74)	4.64** (1.95)	0.44 (2.55)
Order taxcred, other2	2.80*** (0.94)	2.12** (0.65)	2.54** (0.94)	−0.40 (1.04)	−0.71 (1.09)	0.05 (0.32)
Order sub, other2	5.43*** (1.24)	2.33** (0.86)	2.84** (0.91)	0.18 (0.83)	0.11 (0.65)	0.04 (0.32)
Order envtax, other2	0.26 (0.53)	0.84* (0.44)	0.36 (0.36)	0.11 (1.11)	0.61 (0.61)	0.032 (0.08)
Repeated						
Repeated_ taxcred	1.58 (0.30)	1.30 (0.49)	−0.34 (0.53)	0.89 (0.57)	0.16 (0.58)	−0.225 (0.19)
Repeated_sub	1.63*** (0.44)	0.93 (0.55)	0.67 (0.60)	1.33** (0.80)	0.34 (0.18)	−0.49 (0.43)
Repeated_ envtax	0.54 (0.17)	0.55 (0.57)	0.50 (0.47)	0.82 (0.84)	0.27 (0.14)	0.193 (0.08)
At once						
At_once taxcred, sub	Omitted	Omitted	Omitted	Omitted	Omitted	Omitted
At_once taxcred, envtax	8.45*** (0.70)	3.82*** (0.50)	1.60*** (0.66)	0.08 (0.86)	0.084* (1.09)	0.01 (0.04)
At_once envtax, sub	−0.38* (0.20)	−1.57 (1.15)	−1.33 (1.18)	−3.57** (0.99)	−0.06 (0.05)	0.72 (0.47)
Once						
Taxcred	1.04 (0.49)	−0.49 (0.57)	0.86* (0.40)	−0.30 (0.47)	−0.46* (0.25)	−0.45 (0.15)
Envtax	0.02 (0.31)	−0.05 (0.52)	−0.04 (0.29)	−0.36 (0.31)	−0.71 (0.21)	0.18 (0.12)

(Continued)

Table 5.3 (Continued)

	avglnCP (1)	*avglnCPair* (2)	*avglnCPenc* (3)	*avglnEP* (4)	*avglnEPair* (5)	*avgllnRD* (6)
Sub	1.73*** (0.49)	0.52 (0.36)	1.29** (0.40)	0.42 (0.47)	0.22 (0.18)	0.18 (0.15)
Controls	×	×	×	×	×	×
Firm FE	×	×	×	×	×	×
Year FE	×	×	×	×	×	×
R-squared	0.19	0.07	0.02	0.23	0.08	0.02
N	23,115	23,115	23,115	23,111	23,115	23,115

(*Source*: Tchorzewska et al., 2025)

Notes: Each coefficient is estimated from different regressions following the main specification. Additional controls are firm size, sector, and year dummies as well as green employees, environmental certifications, and lagged investment. Standard errors in parentheses are clustered at the firm level. $*p < 0.1$, $**p < 0.05$, and $***p < 0.01$.

compliance-related technology, and among firms subject to highest tax intensity. For CP, weak or moderate levies rarely clear internal investment hurdles by themselves. The underlying incentives are sufficiently salient, certain, or bankable to trigger capital expenditure in the absence of complementary finance. In that sense, taxation alone tends to reshape the composition of investment at the margin, rather than generating broad-based new projects.

The policy mix of tax plus aid performs strongly in the broad comparison of "both versus none": CP and EP investments both rise sharply, illustrating complementarity, a price signal that makes savings valuable combined with capital support that lowers first costs and risk. The results are dose-dependent. At low and medium tax intensities, layering a tax on top of aid adds the most; showing that only with the grant or allowance, even small environmental tax can bring most projects over the line. At high tax intensity, by contrast, the mix does not add value. It seems when environmental tax bite is substantial, complementing it with public aid for investment, does not result in any further deepening or acceleration into efficiency upgrades.

This asymmetry yields an interesting design message. Where the primary objective is energy efficiency via cleaner production, regulators should start by relieving first costs through targeted capital support or accelerated allowances and anchor those investments in a credible, durable price signal on energy or emissions. Weak environmental taxes layered on top of financial aid tend to materially shift investment behaviour already. Targeting should prioritise firms most constrained by their balance sheets, for example, small and medium-sized enterprises (SMEs) and plants with thin cash flows; and disbursement should be tied to verified performance in terms of energy savings or emissions reductions, rather than mere eligibility.

Thus, we have answered the second research question of this chapter, showing that policy-mixes seem to work best at driving green technology adoption at low to medium levels of environmental taxation. At high levels of environmental taxation, the addition of subsidy does not increase green technology uptake any further.

5.2.4 Difference-in-difference analysis

Where institutional features permit, difference-in-differences (DiD) designs can substantially sharpen identification of green fiscal policy-mix effects (Wang et al., 2023; Zhao et al., 2023; Zhou et al., 2022). Ma et al. (2023) provide a clear two-step template for evaluating a static policy-mix: it first applies DiD to estimate the effect of China's Green Credit Guidelines (2012) on firm-level high-quality environmental innovation, and then extends it to a triple-differences design (DDD) to test whether government subsidies amplify or attenuate that effect. The setting is well- suited to this approach because the guidelines were issued nationally to banks but targeted credit tightening towards firms in pre-defined high-polluting industries, leaving other sectors comparatively unaffected, which yields a natural treated–control contrast at the industry level. Firm and year fixed effects absorb time-invariant heterogeneity and common shocks, key regressors are lagged to mitigate simultaneity, and event–time evidence shows no differential pre-trends prior to 2012, supporting the parallel-trends assumption underpinning identification.

The outcome is the natural log of one plus the number of green invention patent applications at the firm–year level. Hence, the baseline DiD is:

$$Ln\left(1+\ GIP\right)_{it}=\alpha_0+\alpha_1 Post_{it}-1+\alpha_2 X_{it}-1+f_i+f_t+\epsilon_{it} \quad (5.5)$$

Where in model specification (5.5), $Post_{\ it-1}$ equals 1 for firms in high-polluting industries after the 2012 guideline (and 0 otherwise), X_{it-1} is a vector of lagged-firm controls (size, age, leverage, profitability, asset mix, ownership, board structure, etc.), η_i are firm fixed effects, and τ_t are year fixed effects. To study the policy-mix with fiscal support, the difference-in-difference-in-difference (DDD) augments the design with the firm's lagged subsidy receipt, $Sub_{\ it-1}$, and its interaction with treatment:

$$Ln\left(1+\ GIP\right)_{it}=\alpha_0+\beta_1 Post_{it}-1+\beta_2 Sub_{\{it-1\}}+\beta_3\left(Post_{\{it-1\}}*Sub_{\{it-1\}}\right)$$
$$+\beta_4 X_{\{it-1\}}+f_i+f_t+\epsilon_{it} \quad (5.6)$$

Here, in equation (5.6), β_1 is the average effect of the credit-screening policy on high-quality green invention among high-polluters; β_3 is the policy-mix term indicating whether subsidies moderate (mitigate or strengthen) the

Green Credit Guidelines' (GCGs') impact. The combination of nationwide timing, industry-based targeting, firm and year fixed effects, lagged covariates, and pre-trend checks makes the DiD/DDD a natural and credible strategy not only for a static policy-mix but also for policy-mixes that develop of time. The empirical specification follows the empirical firm-level literature, including controls for size, age, leverage, profitability (Return on Assets (ROA)), growth, cash holdings, the fixed-asset ratio, ownership concentration, state ownership, and board size, all lagged one period. The key DiD assumption is that, absent the policy, treated and comparison firms would have followed parallel trends in high-quality green invention.

The strengths of this approach are as follows. Under the standard DiD assumptions, it delivers clean causal claims about the effect of tightened green credit on high-quality environmental invention, thus offers high internal validity and external validity. The moderation term then speaks directly to policy complementarity, quantifying how subsidies alter the credit-induced response. The focus on invention patents, and robustness to granted inventions and forward citations, strengthens the interpretation of results as shifts in substantive innovation capacity rather than in low-quality patenting. Extensive, lagged firm-level controls for financial health and governance further reduce omitted-variable bias, which is crucial in a setting where access to green credit and the propensity to patent are both correlated with balance-sheet strength and managerial quality.

The limitations are, however, still there. Firm and time fixed effects, combined with the rich set of lagged controls, mitigate but do not remove requirement of parallel trends, so event–time plots and placebo exercises are indispensable diagnostics. Lagging both the treatment (exposure to the 2012 Green Credit Guidelines, GCGs) and the subsidy moderator one period reduces simultaneity, innovation responding contemporaneously to policy, but cannot fully rule out anticipation (e.g., firms bringing filings forward around the announcement). Identification of the interaction between credit and subsidies is essentially static. The design compares firms under credit with or without subsidies, rather than tracing the sequence of instruments over time. It cannot distinguish whether subsidies deployed prior to tighter credit standards are more effective than subsidies that follow nor whether the moderating effect varies with the intensity of either instrument, such as the subsidy rate or the effective cost of capital under GCGs. Moreover, within the context of green technology adoption, high-quality green patents are still one step removed from the adoption of CP technologies. Diffusion inside plants and associated energy–intensity outcomes may lag or differ in magnitude.

5.3 Does the order of the green fiscal policy-mix matter?

5.3.1 Sequential analysis

Sequential analysis is a brand new concept, first developed and adapted in a working paper by Lenihan et al. (2025b) to study the R&D tax-credits' effects on general innovation and adapted by Tchorzewska et al. (2025) for the first time to uncover the eco-innovation effects of green fiscal policy sequencing. It is a natural extension for policy-mix evaluation because it moves the question from "does instrument A or B matter?" to "in what order do A and B work best?" The procedure treats the policy-mix as a dynamic treatment regime and asks whether particular sequences of instruments are associated with systematically different investment outcomes, conditional on rich fixed effects and controls. In practice, the approach proceeds in three steps and we will explain it on a study carried out by Tchorzewska et al. (2025).

First, the analyst defines a finite set of policy sequences of interest, for example, a tax signal followed by an investment tax credit, or a subsidy followed by a tax credit and then an environmental tax; as well as an exposure window within which those events must occur to count as a sequence. In that application, authors construct two windows: a conservative five-year window and a more permissive three-year window for robustness. Both windows impose strict exclusion zones—no relevant instruments in the two years before the sequence begins—so the valid occurrences are fewer but cleaner.

Second, the analyst codes these sequences into a vector Y_{it} of time-varying indicators or intensities at the firm–year level, alongside standard time-varying controls Z_{it} (lagged investment, sector, size, number of green employees, environmental certifications) and firm and year fixed effects. The baseline specification is:

$$investment_{it} = \sum_{j}^{J} \beta_1 Z_{itj} + \beta_2 Y_{itj} + \alpha_t + \alpha_i + \varepsilon_{it} \tag{5.7}$$

where the outcome is the firm's expenditure on technology adoption or environmental R&D, averaged over the designated time window. The authors estimate equation (5.7) on the treated sample. Firms that received at least one instrument over 2010–2020. This restriction is deliberate—by conditioning on ever-treated firms, one can absorb persistent selection into "ability to obtain support" into the firm fixed effect α_i, so the β_2 coefficients identify within-firm deviations associated with the timing and order of instruments rather than with time-invariant propensity to be supported.

Tchorzewska et al. (2025) estimate effects using forward-looking investment outcomes averaged over five years (main) and three years (robustness). The longer window admits fewer valid sequences, so estimates are conservative; conditional on firm and time fixed effects and controls, the design asks whether particular instrument sequences within a defined window are associated with higher subsequent green investment (average investment across the policy window).

The main advantage of this empirical strategy is that sequential analysis is structurally aligned with the dynamic nature of the policy-mix problem. It recognises that instruments rarely arrive in isolation and delivers estimates that speak directly to ordering—for example, whether a price signal followed by a capital incentive outperforms the reverse. Relative to single-instrument designs, the approach is straightforward to implement with administrative data, nests naturally within fixed-effects panels, and does not depend on strong instruments or sharp thresholds that are often unavailable. Focusing on ever-treated firms differences out persistent selection into support, while temporal exclusion windows reduce contamination from overlapping programmes.

The main caveat is that selection and endogeneity are mitigated only to a certain extent. Programme managers may still time or layer support for firms that are already ramping up investment, and if such time-varying unobservables correlate with the chosen sequence, sequence coefficients remain biased. Additionally, the approach is still information-intensive, requiring granular data. Mismeasurement of exposure will attenuate sequence effects. Results might also be sensitive to the window choice. Wider windows reduce overlap but shrink the sample and statistical power; narrower windows enlarge the sample but increase the risk of programme overlap. Lastly, external validity is still uncertain. By design, never-treated firms are excluded, so estimates capture marginal sequencing effects among actors already inside the policy system, and they average across heterogeneous macro- and sectoral contexts unless explicit interactions are modelled.

A credible implementation therefore hinges on careful exposure construction and parsimonious sequencing rules, with pre-specified windows (five-year baseline, three-year check) and a fixed-effects structure augmented by lagged outcomes, sector–year dummies, and input-price controls. Given many sequences, interpretation should emphasise effect sizes and uncertainty intervals, and where quasi-experimental variation exists for one element, hybrid designs (e.g., instrumenting one instrument while conditioning on the other's timing) can strengthen causal interpretation.

In Table 5.3, we can see five-year investment averages in a firm–year fixed-effects specification, which yield three robust patterns. First, "carrots" increase (CP effectively, when followed by "sticks." When a subsidy or tax credit precedes environmental taxation, CP spendings—especially in energy-saving technologies—are larger; when the order is reversed, the effect fades. Stand-alone subsidies are strongly associated with higher CP expenditure, and this effect persists when subsidies recur. By contrast, tax credits alone are only weakly related to CP, and primarily within energy-efficiency projects, a pattern consistent with the mid-period phase-out of Spain's environmental investment tax credit and the sensitivity of take-up to tax capacity.

Second, policy durability matters more than one-off nudges. Repeated exposure to an instrument, particularly to environmental taxation, is associated with higher investment in energy-efficient CP. Persistence makes savings more salient and reduces the perceived risk of policy reversal. In practical terms, durability functions less as a one-time incentive and more as a capability. Firms re-organise measurement, planning, and supplier relationships when the signal is believed to be credible over time.

Third, not all mixes behave as complements. Pairing subsidy and tax credit (in either order) is associated with lower CP investment than in the absence of external finance, consistent with crowding-out or timing mismatch, and with capital support absent a credible price signal diverting activity towards EP compliance or non-energy projects with weaker cash-flow savings. The EP results align. Subsidies (single and repeated) raise EP investment, tax credits alone appear ineffective, and when tax and subsidy coincide EP investment falls, consistent with fiscal-calendar bunching or a pivot from EP treatment towards prevention at source.

A significant mechanism that helps to organise those findings is such that under the certainty of increasing stringency of regulation, subsidies/tax credits lower the cost of capital and buy time to build capabilities, while subsequent taxation locks in consistent signal of the environmental stringency and returns once projects are operational. While under no strict environmental stringency, piling grants, scholarships, and tax credits for green technology adoption, does not result in any significant deepening of investment, on the contrary it results in smaller investments.

Key limitations remain. Without clean exogenous shocks, sequencing estimates are still best interpreted as strong conditional correlations rather than definitive causality, and further progress likely requires sharper institutional variation or structural approaches. Substantively, extending outcomes from investment to metered performance and productivity (e.g., energy and emissions intensity, employment, assets, and revenues) would help identify mixes that raise CapEx (Capital Expenditure) without improving efficiency or productivity.

For policy design, the central implication is that sequencing is crucial. Process-integrated CP typically requires upfront finance combined with a credible, durable price signal, while EP investment follows compliance timetables and is less responsive to mixes unless linked to performance-based procurement or recovery schemes. Above all, durability matters—repetition lowers perceived risk and raises returns to private effort—suggesting that fiscal instruments should be calibrated in both level and sequence to the frictions highlighted by the energy-efficiency gap and the double externality in eco-innovation. Thus, we have answered the last research question of this chapter, showing that the order of green fiscal policy instruments matters greatly for green technology adoption.

5.4 Conclusions

A unifying theme of this chapter is that no single empirical design can, on its own, resolve the complexity of green fiscal policy evaluation. Fixed-effects models, complementarity analysis, categorical treatment matching, DiD, and sequential analysis each illuminate different challenges of the problem.

This chapter also answers the three research questions. The policy-mix of environmental tax with investment subsidy/tax credit is successful at driving green technology adoption (thus a complement) under the right green fiscal policy design. The instrument dose also matters for the green fiscal policy-mix. We can see that combinations of small to medium environmental tax with investment subsidies drive green technology adoption, while at high levels of environmental taxation the synergistic effect disappears. Lastly and crucially, the order of green fiscal policy instruments seems to matter. Policy tools should be implemented in sequence such that they address the most prevailing barriers first such as capital market failure, thus, the sequential policy-mix of subsidies/tax credits first, environmental tax later is better.

Methodologically, the chapter points to different methods to answer different questions. Fixed-effects and DiD designs offer high internal validity when policy timing is plausibly exogenous, but rely on assumptions about trends and interference. Complementarity tests are conceptually precise yet data-intensive and sensitive to functional form and common support. Categorical treatment matching relaxes parametric structure, aligns well with programme logic, and allows for policy-mixes with different doses, but again it is data intensive and identifies effects primarily for firms already inside the policy system not accounting for unobserved heterogeneity. Sequential analysis, in turn, operationalises the idea that policy-mixes unfold over time rather than appearing instantaneously, but remains exposed to time-varying selection and hinges on detailed administrative histories. The most persuasive evaluations combine these tools, using each to probe the weaknesses of the others and answer different research questions, thus, painting the full view from different angles. Fixed effects characterise broad patterns, categorical treatment matching explore regimes, supermodularity tests where identification allow, DiD for sharp reforms, and sequencing for dynamic mixes.

As for policy implications, green fiscal architecture operates through several channels over time—prices, liquidity, and expectations. Credible and durable price signals on energy use or emissions are crucial for anchoring investment incentives and expected returns. Yet, price increases on their own—especially in environments with tight credit—can shrink firms' capacity to undertake high-quality green innovation. This helps explain why environmental taxation in isolation tends to generate only moderate adoption of energy-efficient technologies, whereas its impact rises substantially when paired with subsidies or tax credits, even when environmental taxation is at the lowest rate. Sequencing also appears to matter for firms' uptake of CP technologies. A pattern consistent with the evidence is that easing liquidity constraints first—via subsidies, tax credits, or other support—followed by the gradual introduction (or tightening) of environmental taxes leads to markedly stronger adoption than the reverse ordering. Frontloading finance and information, and only then phasing in more stringent taxation, seems to encourage more process-integrated cleaner production, while poorly timed or overlapping measures can create administrative delays, crowd out private effort, and shift investment towards lower-quality or purely compliance-oriented upgrades. At the same time, overly generous subsidies or tax credits—regardless of order—may themselves crowd out green technology adoption by replacing private investment.

With regards to the further work, rich administrative data and advances in causal inference should now allow environmental fiscal policies to be studied with a degree of granularity that matches their institutional complexity. The next steps involve following instruments from innovation to adoption, investigating firm behaviour under different policy-mixes when one of the instruments is phased-out (we will try to accomplish this in Chapter 6), and extending the analysis to other firm-level productivity measures—to make clear that the policy-mixes maintain firm competitiveness, and possibly increase it (OECD, 2025b; Yamazaki, 2017). The sequential analysis could be accompanied by other methods or the model could still be extended to control for exogenous changes happening over time, and answering questions on how they interact with macro conditions and sectoral opportunities. Ultimately, investigating precisely, which combinations of green fiscal policy instruments, at which doses and in which order, address the specific frictions that reduce the energy-efficiency gap and slow low-carbon innovation.

6 Empirical analysis

Which policies could help mitigate the negative effects when the Environmental Investment (EI) tax credit is eliminated?

6.1 Introduction

In the pursuit of aligning economic growth with ecological sustainability, firms have increasingly directed their attention to environmental innovation (Acemoglu et al., 2012), also through the adoption of cleaner-production (CP) technology. Subsidies and other fiscal incentives have emerged as crucial facilitators in this transition. Within subsidies, environmental investment tax credits offer a more accessible and cost-effective means of support at the administrative level compared to traditional subsidy funds (Böhringer et al., 2019). The frequent policy changes causing unexpected discontinuation of market-based instruments such as green investment tax credits prompt critical questions regarding its potential repercussions on firms' investment behaviours and, consequently, the trajectory of environmental innovation. Up-to-date research has not sufficiently engaged with behavioural change and co-evolutionary characteristics of low-carbon transition (Matos et al., 2022), this study aims to fill this gap.

In the following empirical work, we consider the so-called process eco-innovations, which can either tackle environmental objectives alone by abating pollution at the end of the production pipe (end-of-pipe (EP) technologies) or change the production process and thus reduce the use of natural resources, energy use, and thus pollution created (process-integrated CP technologies; Frondel et al., 2007). Government regulators, recognising the importance to incentivise environmental technologies, frequently employ subsidies (De Groote & Verboven, 2019; Xie et al., 2019). This strategy is underpinned by the double externality argument (Rennings, 2000) that we have analysed more precisely in Chapter 3, which posits that public subsidies address the environmental externality of carbon dioxide (CO_2) emissions from fossil fuels and a technology market failure. This failure is characterised by a socially suboptimal level of private investment in green technology due to knowledge spillovers, imitation costs, and uncertainty surrounding these technologies (McHenry, 2009). What is more, Greco et al. (2022) show that providing general support for innovation to firms already benefiting from environmental

DOI: 10.4324/9781003712398-6

policies does not create any additional effects on process eco-innovations. This could mean that environmental market failure is larger than the market failure arising from the public-good nature of new knowledge, and that environmental policies indirectly affect Research and Development (R&D), thus possibly no complementarity exists.

This study pioneers an exploration into the behavioural implications of eliminating the Environmental Investment (EI) tax credit for firms investing in green technology adoption (process eco-innovation). To achieve this objective, we use a confidential dataset obtained from the National Institute of Statistics of Spain (INE), derived from the Survey on Industry Expenditure on Environmental Protection (SIEEP) spanning the years 2010–2020 and comprising nearly 37,000 firm–year observations, from which we identify firms that received the EI tax credit once and several times. Employing a panel fixed-effects methodology, specifically employing difference-in-difference (DiD) and event-study methods also in a heterogeneous context, we designate the elimination year as 2015. The treatment group is defined as firms receiving the tax credit more than once, while the control group comprises firms qualifying for the tax credit only once. This approach, by focusing on treatment intensity, controls for self-selection issues. Ultimately, we may observe how firms heavily reliant on the tax credit face its phase-out. Our scrutiny encompasses direct effects on technology adoption, including superior CP technologies and inferior EP technologies, and indirect effects on environmental R&D. Beyond immediate consequences on technology adoption; our investigation delves into unintended outcomes and potential mitigating factors, for example, green employees, using subsidies and paying environmental taxes at a low level.

Spain is an especially well suited setting for this type of empirical analysis. First, and most importantly, it offers a rare case in which a mature Environmental Investment (EI) tax credit was in place for many years and then fully phased out, creating a suitable difference-in-differences setup. Second, the fiscal autonomy of the Autonomous Communities means that regions are free to introduce and design their own environmental taxes, generating substantial heterogeneity in environmental tax implementation and rates, which is exogenous. As a result, otherwise similar firms in our sample face different effective environmental tax burdens purely because they are located in different regions. Third, as summarised in Table 6.1, Spain is broadly representative of other European countries in terms of the existence and scope of green fiscal policy instruments. Both Belgium and Denmark, for instance, have offered tax credits for energy-efficient and sustainable investments (around 13.5% and 16%, respectively), and all countries in the table provide subsidies for green technology adoption. Moreover, all European countries rely on some form of carbon pricing, either via the European Union Emissions Trading System (EU ETS) or through more specific environmental taxes on air or water pollution. Taken together, these features support both the internal validity of

Table 6.1 The existence, scope, and examples of environmental taxes/carbon pricing, tax credits for green technology adoption, and subsidies/grants for green technology adoption existing in different European countries

Country	*Environmental taxes/carbon pricing*	*Tax credits for green technology adoption*	*Subsidies for green technology adoption*
Spain	Environmental, energy taxes on electricity and fossil fuels, vehicle and other transport-related taxes. Environmental taxes at the regional levels. EU ETS	Environmental Investment (EI) tax credit for environmental investments (around 10%, later 8%). Eliminated in 2015. R&D and technological innovation tax credits.	Substantial grants for renewables, energy efficiency, and industrial decarbonisation, largely channelled through the National Recovery and Resilience Plan, PERTE (strategic project for economic recovery and transformation) industrial decarbonisation projects, IDAE (Institute for the Diversification and Saving of Energy) programmes, and EU funds (also for SME).
Belgium	Environmental tax structure with excise duties on energy products and electricity, transport-related taxes and various regional environmental charges. EU ETS	An investment deduction regime for certain assets, including environmentally friendly R&D investments and green technologies (13.5%).	Broad range of regional and federal support schemes for energy efficiency, renewable energy, and innovation (e.g., grants, soft loans, and guarantees). Instruments target both generic innovation and explicitly green projects.
Denmark	Long-standing energy and CO_2 taxes and a recent green tax reform that increases effective CO_2-equivalent tax rates. EU ETS	Between 2020 and 2022, the country introduced a tax credit of 16% for eligible capital investments (green).	Use of grants and tenders to promote renewables, district heating, power-to-X, and industrial energy efficiency. Multiple schemes administered by the Danish Energy Agency and supported by EU.
Germany	Energy tax and electricity tax, complemented since 2021 by the national emissions trading system (nEHS) for heating and transport fuels. EU ETS	Accelerated depreciation for certain climate-related investments alongside a relatively generous R&D tax incentive that can include low-carbon technologies.	Substantial grant and soft-loan programmes for energy and resource efficiency, renewables, and industrial decarbonisation (e.g., federal industrial decarbonisation schemes, carbon-contracts-for-difference pilots and KfW (Credit Institute for Reconstruction) credit lines).

(Continued)

Table 6.1 (Continued)

Country	*Environmental taxes/carbon pricing*	*Tax credits for green technology adoption*	*Subsidies for green technology adoption*
Poland	Excise taxes on liquid, gaseous, and solid fuels plus electricity, vehicle and transport-related charges. Additional environmental fees for waste disposal, water use, river/coastal discharges, air pollution, paid at the regional level. EU ETS	General R&D tax relief and temporary state-aid frameworks that may include tax advantages for certain zero-carbon and energy-efficiency projects.	Growing mix of loans and grants for renewables and energy-efficiency investments, including the Ecological Credit (Kredyt Ekologiczny) for energy-saving projects and various EU-funded schemes under programmes such as FENG (European Funds for a Modern Economy).
Sweden	Very high carbon tax on fossil fuels outside the EU ETS (about Swedish krona (SEK) 1,510 per tonne of CO_2 in 2025), combined with energy and vehicle taxes. EU ETS	General R&D incentives and standard depreciation rules	Extensive grant and soft-loan schemes for industrial decarbonisation, innovation, and green infrastructure (e.g., industrial transformation programmes and green industrial policy packages), often co-funded with EU resources. These support large industrial projects and technology demonstrations.
United Kingdom	A carbon-pricing and environmental tax system (UK ETS, CCL on business energy use and others).	Tax relief is mainly provided through capital allowances and, more recently, full expensing for qualifying plant and machinery, which can include energy-efficient and low-carbon equipment.	A range of competitive grant schemes for industrial decarbonisation and energy efficiency, such as the Industrial Energy Transformation Fund and various innovation competitions, alongside regional and sector-specific support for low-carbon technologies.

Source: self-made

our identification strategy and the external validity of our results for other European contexts.

Overall, the findings reveal persistent negative effects of EI-tax credit elimination on investment in superior process-integrated energy-efficient technologies, but not on compliance driven inferior pollution-abating technologies. However, evidence also shows that under the right policy mix and firm organisational capabilities, for example, by drawing on subsidies, paying low-level environmental taxes, and hiring green employees can partially and even fully compensate for the loss of the tax credit. More specifically, results indicate that eliminating green technology policies differs on whether a firm was located in an Autonomous Community (AC) in which an environmental tax is present, and varied through their internal adaptive strategies. Focusing on the 2015 phase-out of the Environmental Investment (EI) tax credit in Spain, we observe that firms heavily reliant on tax credits reduced investments in superior, CP technologies while maintaining levels of inferior EP technologies. Interestingly, these firms also temporarily intensified investments in private environmental R&D, showcasing adaptability to policy changes and flexible movement of resources. Small firms are particularly affected, as those firms struggle more with capital market failure. Mitigation strategies include, for example, utilising subsidies instead. It also seems that hiring green employees shields the firm from negative investment, while on the regulator side, if a firm needs to pay a small level of environmental taxation that already ensures its non-reduction in green technology adoption. Acknowledging study limitations such as relatively small sample size, our results underscore the lasting negative impacts of EI tax-credit elimination, emphasising the need for careful policy considerations in the green technology landscape.

The remainder of the chapter is structured as follows. Section 6.2 discusses the empirical literature. Section 6.3 describes the institutional setting, data, and the methodologies used; Section 6.4 discusses the results, and Section 6.5 develops the analysis by adding extensions and robustness checks. Section 6.6 concludes and reports our policy recommendations. All the tables are provided at the end of the chapter.

6.2 Literature review

6.2.1 Eco-innovation

Green technology adoption, also known in the literature as eco-innovation, is driven by internal and external factors (del Río et al., 2021; Horbach, 2008; Horbach et al., 2013). The internal factors include technological competency, organisational capabilities, knowledge, skills, customer relationships, and green employees (García-Quevedo et al., 2022; Demirel & Kesidou, 2011; Jové-Llopis & Segarra-Blasco, 2018; Pujari, 2006; Ying et al., 2022). Parrilli et al. (2023) show that science-driven and practice-driven strategies drive eco-innovation at the firm level. In contrast, the external factors include regulatory pressure (e.g., command and control) and a range of market-based instruments, such as environmental taxes, subsidies, tax credits, etc. Scholars underline that given the "sluggish diffusion of green technologies," the external factors are especially crucial in the transition towards a sustainable economy (Hötte, 2020). With regards to regulatory pressure, Zhang et al. (2024) find on a sample of manufacturing firms in China that with an exogenous shock of environmental policy, firms in regulated industries tend to develop services. Along this line, Donis et al. (2023) underline the economic complexity and strength of patents (intellectual property rights) that positively drive eco-innovation.

Interestingly, the literature also shows that external factors can affect the adoption of green technologies differently, depending on their inherent characteristics. Frondel et al. (2007) make a distinction between integrated CP technologies and solely pollution-abating technologies (commonly known as end-of-pipe), given the different characteristics they entail. EP addresses the environmental objectives alone and bears no efficiency and economic benefits, for example, filters and sulphur scrubbers. Firms also consider them as costly investments that could potentially trigger the loss of competitiveness. Despite this, they are preferred due to lower fixed investment costs compared to the alternative—CP technologies. In contrast, CP technologies change the production process and use natural resources more efficiently, and through that, they reduce the amount of emissions created and thus also emitted. Thus, they aim both at environmental objectives and cost efficiency (Carraro et al., 2010; Demirel & Kesidou, 2011, p. 2019). Ultimately, literature has acknowledged in the last 15 years that since eco-innovations have different characteristics, they have also different drivers (De Marchi, 2012; García-Quevedo et al., 2022; Haller & Murphy, 2012; Horbach et al., 2012; Triguero et al., 2013).

6.2.2 Subsidies and eco-innovation

The literature so far has underlined that market-based instruments are much more effective than command-and-control (CAC) regulations, and within market-based instruments, environmental taxes are preferred because they allow firms to use private information on the best technology to adopt while directly internalising the cost of climate change into the market prices. With regards to subsidies, despite the economic justification and their widespread implementation, there is limited empirical evidence on the effectiveness of subsidies designed to stimulate green technology adoption. Scholars mostly agree that they result in higher eco-innovation levels for most countries (Cainelli & Mazzanti, 2013; Horbach, 2008; Horbach et al., 2012; Hu et al., 2021; Xie et al., 2019; Li et al., 2022). There is, however, scant evidence that subsidies might not be very relevant (Rave et al., 2011). Additionally, subsidies are sometimes criticised for helping financial firms that would have innovated anyway (crowding-in vs. crowding-out described in the context of R&D

subsidies in Marino et al. (2016). This is relevant since governments distribute considerable public resources through public financing of green technologies through subsidies and tax credits. Subsidies might perform differently depending on the characteristics of competing technologies (Garcia-Quevedo & Jove-Llopis, 2021; García-Quevedo et al., 2022). Moreover, information asymmetries on firm profiles and their environmental projects may also hinder an efficient allocation of subsidies (Zhang, 2022; Wu et al., 2022).

In the Spanish context, subsidies are effective (Arranz et al., 2019; De Marchi, 2012; Peñasco et al., 2017). What has been consistently shown is that small firms benefit the most from green subsidies because they may reduce the financial barriers to innovation through them (del Río et al., 2017). Additionally, García-Quevedo et al. (2022) provided empirical evidence that green investment subsidies lead to higher investments into CP and EP technologies. But the works by Triguero et al. (2013), Jové-Llopis and Segarra-Blasco (2018), and Cuerva et al. (2014) found contrasting evidence. Finally, a study by Wu et al. (2022) indiced that subsidies given to energy firms might follow an inverted U-shaped curve for innovation, pointing to an optimal point of subsidy provision. Along this line, a working paper by Marino et al. (2024) using data in a Dutch context shows that as the level of the subsidy increases, firms move their resources towards inferior EP technologies.

6.2.3 *Tax credits and eco-innovation*

Green fiscal incentives have been investigated much less frequently, even though they are easier and cheaper to implement at the administrative level (Böhringer et al., 2019) and ultimately provide more flexibility in the technology chosen. Consequently, a precise design of the tax credit in place is necessary not to finance technologies considered inferior and already required through environmental regulations. We have found a handful of empirical papers investigating green investment tax credits. Long and Liao (2021) provide empirical evidence that subsidies and tax credits are positively associated with green product innovation. However, within the effects of green tax credits on the diffusion of green technologies among manufacturing firms, Garcia-Quevedo et al. (2022) show that tax credits (deductions on corporate income taxes) result in a higher investment in CP technologies in Spain. More specifically, the authors found that only 3% of companies use tax credits (a similar percentage at of subsidies), yet the amount of money received through this tax credit was three times higher.

6.2.4 *The effects of modifications and eliminations of subsidies/tax credits*

Empirical evidence on how firms adjust when subsidies or tax credits are reformed or withdrawn is scarce; most related work sits in the energy production domain (Chronopoulos et al., 2016). Hagspiel et al. (2021) develop a theoretical model of potential feed-in-tariff (FIT) retraction and show that the set of FIT levels under which immediate investment is optimal shrinks the longer the subsidy has been in place; when the FIT is low and/or long-standing, firms optimally delay investment until after withdrawal and profitable market conditions emerge. Nagy et al. (2021) similarly find that a higher perceived probability of withdrawal induces firms to accelerate investment, but often at the cost of smaller project size. Using a Computable Green Equilibrium (CGE) counterfactual, Jia and Lin (2021) report that removing a cross-subsidy can improve economic performance while worsening CO_2 emissions, industrial structure, and social welfare. A parallel literature examines the removal of fossil-fuel subsidies (Antimiani et al., 2023; Arzaghi & Squalli, 2023), but this work also relies largely on ex-ante dynamic CGE simulations rather than ex-post empirical evaluations.

Empirical evidence on policy uncertainty and subsidy retractions is limited and concentrated in the energy sector, where studies generally find statistically significant, negative effects on investment (Lüthi & Wüstenhagen, 2012; Sendstad et al., 2022). Sendstad et al. (2022), for example, use a country–year panel and a difference-in-differences design to estimate that renewable investment falls by about 45% following a subsidy retraction. Evidence in manufacturing is rarer; Tchorzewska (2024) is the closest study, analysing Spain's Environmental Investment (EI) tax-credit reform in 2011, which aimed to discourage EP financing. She finds the change reduced EP investment, while CP investment was broadly stable, with increases concentrated among the smallest firms. At the same time, her DiD does not model treatment intensity, does not restrict the sample to firms already investing in green technologies (to better address self-selection), and focuses on 2008–2014—prior to the phase-out. Taken together, and given that earlier EI reforms tilted support towards process-integrated technologies, these considerations motivate the conjecture that eliminating the EI tax credit could depress CP investment more than EP investment.

Hypothesis 1: The removal of the Environmental Investment Tax Credits is associated with a decline in cleaner production technologies.

Hypothesis 2: The removal of the Environmental Investment Tax Credit is associated with no negative effect on investment in end-of-pipe technologies.

6.2.5 Indirect effects on environmental R&D

Subsidies and tax credits can reshape firms' perceptions of the complexity and feasibility of adopting new practices, and their innovation responses often depend on firms' broader innovation portfolios (Vasileiou et al., 2024). By lowering factor costs and easing financing constraints, incentives targeted at CP technologies may also stimulate private environmental R&D—an activity that is risky, intangible, and typically distant from commercialisation—particularly when diffusion creates learning-by-doing and learning-by-using opportunities that accelerate technological change through feedback and skill acquisition (Popp, 2006). Empirical evidence is broadly consistent with these channels. Subsidies can foster circular supply-chain management and eco-innovation, with effects shaped by managerial experience (Li et al., 2023), and policy-mixes that support adoption can generate wider eco-innovation benefits (Fischer & Newell, 2008). At the same time, layering generic innovation support onto firms already covered by environmental policy may yield little additional effect on process eco-innovations, suggesting that the environmental market failure may dominate the knowledge public-good failure and that environmental policy can indirectly steer R&D incentives (Greco et al., 2022). Recent work on fiscal instruments aligns with this view. Environmental investment (EI) tax credits in Spain appear to increase environmental investment and indirectly support environmental R&D (Tchorzewska, 2025b), and higher adoption subsidies are associated with indirect increases in environmental R&D, particularly internal R&D, as shown for the Dutch programme (Marino et al., 2024). Evidence is mixed across contexts, however. Subsidies may encourage process-oriented behaviours such as certifications without necessarily raising environmental R&D (Ren et al., 2019). Taken together—and given firms' resource flexibility (Tuominen et al., 2004) and the EI tax credit's orientation towards process-integrated cleaner production—we hypothesise that its elimination may lead firms to reallocate resources towards internal private green R&D.

Hypothesis 3: The removal of the Environmental Investment tax credit may have an indirect, temporary positive effect on environmental R&D.

6.3 Data and methods

In this section, we provide a policy setting and an overview of the data at our disposal and outline the methodologies used, for example, DiD and dynamic DiD, which are used as the identification of the policy change in place. This study uses a unique administrative dataset comprising a comprehensive sample of Spanish industrial firms across the years 2010–2020, totaling almost 37,000 firm–year observations.

6.3.1 Environmental investment tax-credit phase-out

Since joining the European Union (EU), Spain has made significant economic and environmental advancements, with a 18.44% reduction in greenhouse gas (GHG) emissions from 2008 to 2018 (González et al., 2024). However, many challenges remain; for instance, emissions of some pollutants have increased since 2013, e.g., NMVOCs (non-methane volatile organic compounds), NH_3 (ammonia), and others (Vivanco et al., 2021). Even more so, a strategic environmental policy design to ensure a steady transition of the manufacturing industry into energy-efficient and non-carbon–intensive solutions is crucial.

In the early 1990s, the European Commission encouraged member states to adopt environmentally friendly policies. Instead of introducing national environmental taxes, Spain opted for Environmental Investment tax credits (EI tax credits). The EI tax credit, initially established under Law 13/1996 and extended indefinitely by Law 66/1997, targeted eligible environmental protection investments, such as those addressing air, noise, water pollution, and industrial waste. Despite its intent to support CP technologies, the vague legal conditions led firms to increasingly finance EP technologies using the tax incentive (OECD, 2010). The EI tax credit, centralised in its implementation, aimed to induce voluntary investments by reducing costs and payback periods, addressing capital market failures (Zwick & Mahon, 2017). Though used successfully for almost two decades, the government deemed it inefficient arguing that the EI tax credit mostly finances technologies that are already required by the environmental regulation—thus EP, prompting a gradual phase-out from 2006 to 2011 (OECD, 2008).

Surprisingly, after being completely phased out in 2011, the EI tax credit was reintroduced in March 2011 at 8%, emphasising stricter guidelines favouring CP technologies, it was done mostly due to the financial crises and the need to support the manufacturing sector in those challenging times. This sudden reform, intending to support energy-efficient technologies, led to much confusion among the firms. However, four years after the modification, the EI tax credit was ultimately eliminated in 2015 (Law 27/2014), without the proper assessment of the previous modification and its potential benefits. Focusing on industrial firms, this study investigates how the phase-out of the EI tax credit affected firms' investment decisions. Until now, besides positive legal assessments of the existence of the EI tax credit itself (Barreiro Carril, 2015), only one empirical study investigated the effectiveness of this EI tax credit (Tchorzewska, 2024) reaching the conclusion that the modification of 2011 was indeed successful at discouraging financing of EP technologies and encouraging CP technology adoption among the smallest firms.

6.3.2 Data source and variables

This research chapter relies on empirical data sourced from the National Statistics Institute of Spain (INE), extracted from the annual "Survey on Industry Expenditure on Environmental Protection (SIEEP)." The survey serves as a representative source of information for Spanish industrial firms, specifically focusing on collecting data related to environmental protection expenditures. The dataset identifies the primary activity within each firm as the industry contributing the highest added value. The firm-level data span the years 2010–2020.

Table 6.2 Variable definitions

Variable	*Definition*
Dependent variables	
CP	Cleaner production technologies (euros)
lnCP	Natural logarithm of CP + 0.001
ln_netCP	Natural logarithm of CP net of tax credits received in a given year: ln(CP – tax credit + 0.001)
CPair	Cleaner production technologies aimed at air-pollution reduction (euros)
lnCPair	Natural logarithm of CPair + 0.001
ln_netCPair	Natural logarithm of CPair net of tax credits received in a given year: ln(CPair – tax credit + 0.001)
CPenc	Cleaner production technologies aimed at reduction of energy consumption (euros)
lnCPenc	Natural logarithm of CPenc + 0.001
ln_netCPenc	Natural logarithm of CPenc net of tax credits received in a given year: ln(CPenc – tax credit + 0.001)
EP	End-of-pipe technologies (euros)
lnEP	Natural logarithm of EP + 0.001
ln_netEP	Natural logarithm of EP net of tax credits received in a given year: ln(EP – tax credit + 0.001)
EPair	End-of-pipe technologies aimed at air-pollution reduction (euros)
lnEPair	Natural logarithm of EPair + 0.001
ln_netEPair	Natural logarithm of EPair net of tax credits received in a given year: ln(EPair – tax credit + 0.001)

Notes: All logarithms use base e. A small constant (0.001) is added to avoid log of zero.

The INE ensures the data quality through a centralised collection unit responsible for verifying all information in the survey questionnaire. A detailed list of variables and their corresponding definitions is outlined in Table 6.2. Unfortunately, due to confidentiality concerns and restrictions imposed by the INE, integrating this dataset with other sources is not feasible. Nonetheless, it is noteworthy that this survey provides a wealth of pertinent firm characteristics crucial for our analysis, as acknowledged in earlier studies covering the period from 2008 to 2014 (García-Quevedo et al., 2022; Tchorzewska, 2024; Tchórzewska et al., 2022) and 2010–2020 (Tchorzewska et al., 2025).

6.3.3 Dependent variables

Regarding the dependent variables, our primary focus lies in examining the adoption of various green technologies. Definitions for these variables are outlined in Table 6.2. We categorise the technologies in aggregate terms into CP technologies and EP technologies. To enhance the precision of our analysis, we extend our investigation to include more specific measures of green technology adoption. This involves cleaner production technologies aimed at air-pollution reduction (CPair), cleaner production technologies targeted at energy consumption reduction (CPenc), and end-of-pipe technology aimed at air-pollution reduction (EPair). In our analysis, we use those variables net of tax credit received, and in logarithms, thus calculated as ln(net_investment + 0.001), not to exclude observations where investment is equal to 0.

In examining the effects of green technology adoption, we also assess potential spillovers of the EI tax-credit elimination on green innovation at the firm level, proxied by private green R&D. The utilisation of environmental R&D serves two crucial purposes: first, it acts as a robustness check, confirming the authenticity of our results, and second, it enables us to investigate whether the elimination of the EI tax credit indirectly affects environmental R&D, as observed in prior studies. Existing literature has suggested that some firms may redirect funds from environmental subsidies (Marino et al., 2024) and environmental investment tax credits (Tchorzewska, 2025b) towards investments in green R&D.

6.3.4 Descriptive statistics

As mentioned, our full dataset provides unique data on almost 5,800 Spanish industrial firms, accruing to around 37,800 firm–year observations between 2010 and 2020. We use this full dataset for robustness checks. However, given the identification used in this study and the definition of the treatment and control groups, which ensures the highest robustness of results, we limit our dataset to 1,535 firm–year observations, where all firms invest in some kind of green technology every year (d_total_investment = 1) and receive an EI tax credit at least once between 2010 and 2014 (Table 6.3). By doing this, we control for self-selection of firms into investment in green technologies, and self-selection into EI tax-credit use—thus controlling for a large share of firms' unobserved characteristics. The descriptives divided for treatment and control groups are provided in Table 6.3, where treatment is a firm that has used the EI tax credit more than once between 2010 and 2014, and the control group consists of firms that received a tax credit only once in the same time period.

Table 6.3 reveals interesting findings. Firstly, frequent recipients of the EI tax credit demonstrate, on average, higher investments in inferior EP and EPair technologies and CPair cleaner production technologies designed for air-pollution reduction—technologies all mostly aligning with existing environmental regulations. Notably, comparable amounts of money are invested in aggregated CP investments between the treated and control groups. Surprisingly, frequent tax-credit recipients invest significantly less (approximately 50%) in CP targeting energy consumption reduction (energy-efficient technologies) and slightly less in environmental R&D. This suggests that firms utilising the EI tax credit multiple times within a few years tend to prioritise technologies by environmental regulations. Furthermore, frequent tax-credit

Table 6.3 Descriptive statistics for the final sample

	d_highcreditreceivers = 0			*d_highcreditreceivers = 1*		
Variable	*Mean*	*Standard deviation*	*N*	*Mean*	*Standard deviation*	*N*
d_total_investment	1	0	774	1	0	761
ln_net_totainvestment	12.14	2.03	774	12.77	1.98	761
dEP	0.57	0.50	774	0.62	0.49	761
EP	474,116	1,578,345	774	637,382	4,081,809	761
ln_netEP	5.25	8.12	774	7.18	7.66	761
dEPair	0.24	0.43	774	0.29	0.46	761
EPair	177,923	700,461	774	347,967	3,889,799	761
ln_netEPair	−0.26	7.34	774	1.34	7.85	761
dCP	1.0	0	774	1	0	761
CP	1,006,700	3,034,244	774	1,284,239	4,833,135	761
ln_netCP	9.35	6.33	774	10.28	6.14	761
dCPair	0.39	0.49	774	0.51	0.50	761
CPair	458,041	1,981,752	774	814,899	4,430,660	761
ln_netCPair	2.19	8.22	774	5.54	8.42	761
dCPenc	0.36	0.48	774	0.37	0.48	761
CPenc	330,488	1,430,456	774	150,363	637,053	761
ln_netCPenc	1.61	8.05	774	2.77	8.13	761
dRD	0.07	0.26	774	0.10	0.30	761
RD	23,029	231,067	774	19,471	115,120	761
ln_RD	−3.51	3.93	774	−3.17	4.54	761
d_subsidy	0.08	0.26	774	0.13	0.34	761
subsidy	6,732	47,282	774	26,496	20,2678	761
d_envtax	0.42	0.49	774	0.43	0.50	761
envtax	437,125	2,866,172	774	537,634	5,349,072	761
tax_credit	21,610	293,704	774	85,071	574,440	761
Green employees	7.26	12.60	774	6.19	9.22	761
Size	442	971	774	337.39	435.20	761

Notes: Means and standard deviations are reported by high-credit receiver status. N denotes the number of firm–year observations.

recipients tend to be statistically smaller firms, employing, on average, one fewer green employee than firms using the tax credit only once. Lastly, frequent tax-credit recipients are more likely to utilise subsidies (d_subsidy = 0.13 for the treatment group vs. d_subsidy = 0.08 for the control group), while both treatment and control groups face environmental taxation at similar percentages (around 42%).

6.3.5 Empirical design

The lack of eligibility criteria for the Environmental Investment (EI) tax credit introduces the challenge of self-selection bias. To address this concern, we adopt a strategy focusing on treatment intensity. Specifically, we define a treatment group comprising firms that utilised the EI tax credit more than once between 2010 and 2014 and a control group consisting of firms that availed themselves of the tax credit once within the same time frame. Thus, in our main analysis, all firms have received a tax credit at least once and thus invested in green technology at least once. This intensity-based approach enables us to identify firms with the capacity to deduct green investments from the Spanish Corporate Tax, allowing us to study the effect of receiving the treatment multiple times among similar types of firms.

To further control for self-selection, our robustness checks involve a subset of observations where firms invested in some kind of green technology every year. This approach allows us to scrutinise the effect of using the tax credit on increasing the investment amount, differentiating between the extensive (decision to invest) and intensive (investment amount) margins, respectively (Lenihan et al., 2025b).

Additionally, we calculate net investment amounts as our dependent variables for a given firm–year observation, representing the investment in the adoption of a specific technology net of the tax credit received. Since the EI tax credit is proportional to the investment, investigating its proportional effect would be tautological. Instead, we treat the independent variables as dummies, enabling us to examine the additional effect of using a tax credit beyond the proportional impact of the subsidy received.

As a final treatment shock, we take the elimination of the EI tax credit in 2015 from the Spanish Corporate Income Tax. We employ a DiD model to identify the treatment effect, as articulated in Equation (6.1). This approach allows us to disentangle the effects of the EI tax-credit elimination on firms' green technology adoption strategies, considering both the intensity and timing of the treatment.

$$\ln\_outcome_{it} = \delta interaction_{it} + \beta X_{it} + \alpha_i + \alpha_t + \epsilon_{it} \quad (6.1)$$

where in model specification (6.1), i represents the firm identifier and t denotes the observed year for a given firm. The natural logarithm of the outcome variable, ln_outcome, serves as our dependent variable, capturing the net amount of any investment decision undertaken by a firm in a particular year, adjusted for the tax credit received (net of the tax credit received). This encompasses investments in CP and EP technologies in aggregate and more specific amounts.

Specification (6.1) introduces an interaction term between tax-credit treatment intensity and the years in which the policy was phased out where interaction equals to d_high_taxcredit_receiver * post-2015, accounting for the interconnectedness of the treatment with the policy phase-out. The dummy interaction term takes the value of 1 if a given firm received the tax credit more than once in the years 2008–2014, and its investment levels were observed in 2015–2020, and it takes the value of 0 otherwise. The control group consists of firms that received the tax credit only once in 2010–2014. Thus, the coefficient δ in this model represents the DiD estimate, capturing the differential impact of the tax-credit treatment intensity pre- and post phase-out in 2015.

Furthermore, to account for time-invariant unobserved characteristics at the firm level, we incorporate firm-fixed effects (α_i). Additionally, year-fixed effects (α_t) are included to control for time-varying aggregate effects of the business cycle that may affect all firms simultaneously. These fixed effects and our identification strategy provide a robust framework to isolate the specific effects of tax-credit treatment intensity and its interaction with the post-2015 period on the dependent variable, offering a nuanced understanding of the policy's impact over time.

Consequently, we employ a DiD strategy to examine the impact of eliminating the EI tax credit in 2015 on two distinct groups of firms. Those that frequently utilised the tax credit versus those that used it only once. The DiD methodology operates under the assumption that, although there may be unobserved characteristics leading firms to self-select into treated and control groups, as long as their behaviour evolves in parallel, the underlying assumptions are satisfied. As we will see in the event study (Figures 6.1–6.6) for all investments, except for EP and EPair, we do not see any anticipatory effects (no statistically significant coefficients), confirming our parallel-trend assumption. We seem to observe an increase in the use of EP technologies

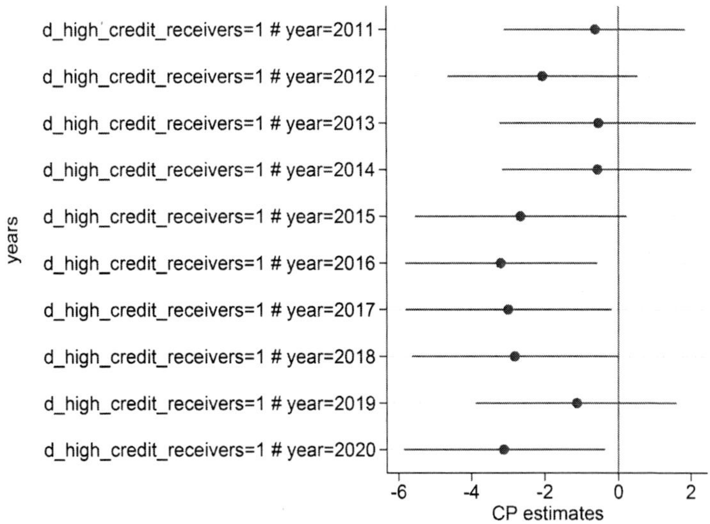

Figure 6.1 Dynamic regression coefficients on investment in cleaner-production technologies (ln_netCP)

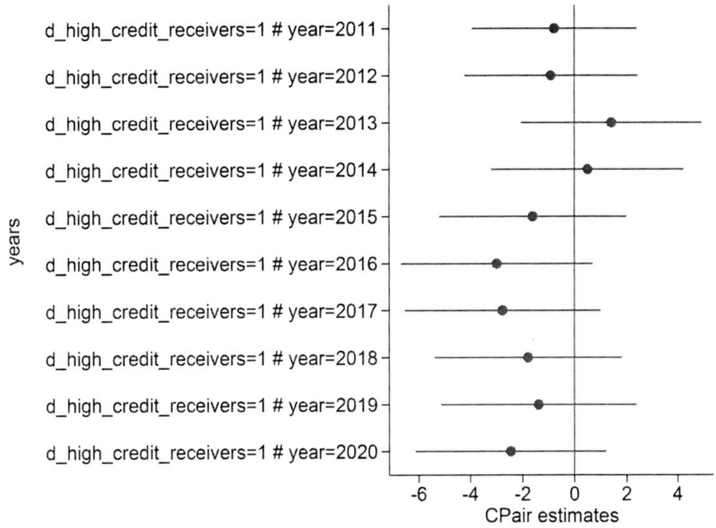

Figure 6.2 Dynamic regression coefficients on investment in cleaner-production technologies aimed at air-pollution reduction (ln_netCPair)

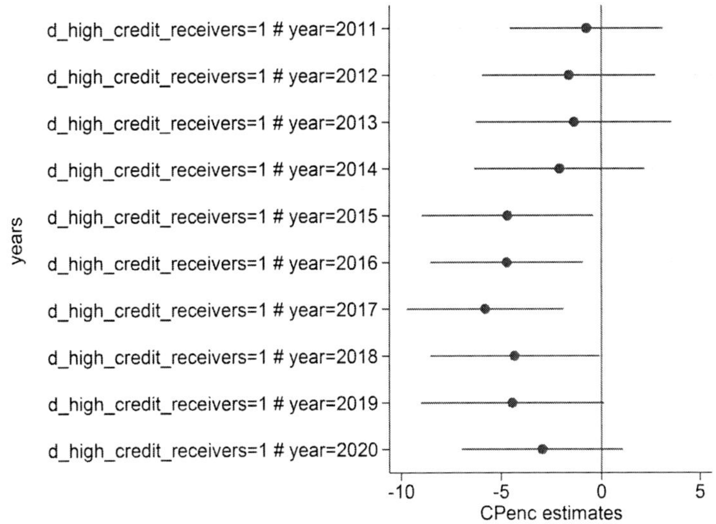

Figure 6.3 Dynamic regression coefficients on investment in cleaner-production technologies aimed at energy consumption reduction (ln_netCPenc)

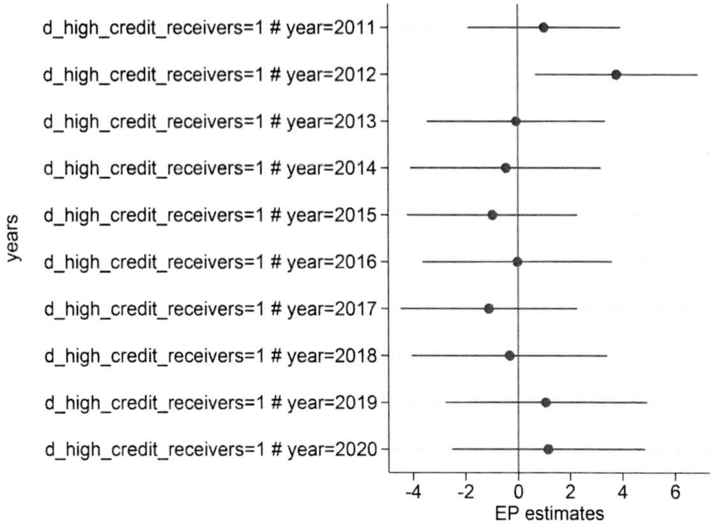

Figure 6.4 Dynamic regression coefficients on investment in end-of-pipe technologies (ln_netEP)

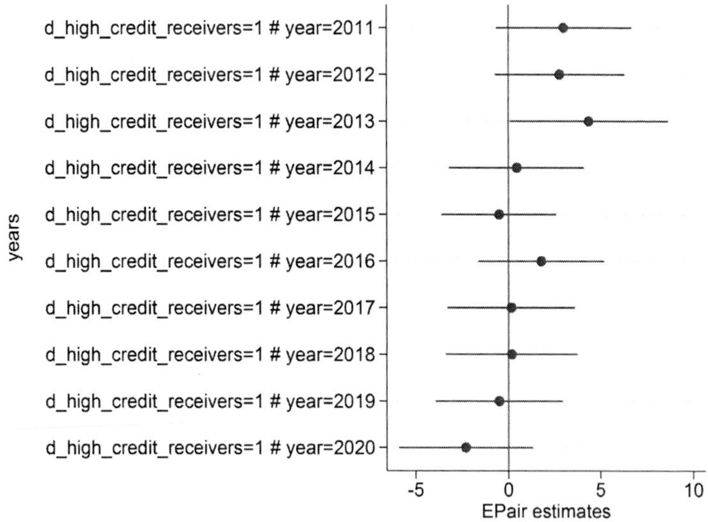

Figure 6.5 Dynamic regression coefficients on investment in end-of-pipe technologies aimed at air-pollution reduction (ln_netEPair)

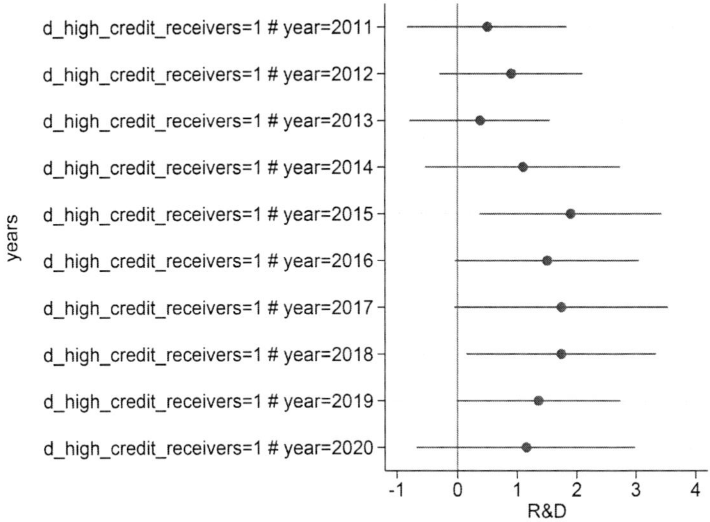

Figure 6.6 Dynamic regression coefficients on investment in private environmental R&D (ln_envRD)

among the frequent users prior to the EI tax-credit phase-out, thus for those technologies we cannot interpret the coefficients as causal.

To provide some sense of the dynamics of the "treatment" effect using our data, I perform an exercise similar in spirit to the analysis in the paper by Autor (2003). The exercise also lends us insights into any behavioural effect that may be present. We do this by replacing the interaction dummy (d_high_taxcredit_receiver*post2015) with a series of lead and lag dummies indicating the time passage relative to the policy implementation.

The specification we consider is the following (6.2):

$$\ln\_outcome_{it} = \sum_{\{T=-q\}}^{\{-1\}} \gamma_T interaction_{it} + \sum_{\{T=0\}}^{\{m\}} \delta_T interaction_{it} + X_{it} + \alpha_i + \alpha_t + \epsilon_{it} \tag{6.2}$$

where treatment occurs in year $T = 0$, gamma coefficients capture the anticipatory effects (through interacting the treatment dummy with a given year prior to the EI tax-credit phase-out), and $q = 4$ (for years, 2011–2014), while the delta coefficients capture the post-treatment effects of the EI tax-credit elimination and $m = 6$ (for years 2015–2020). X is a matrix of control variables at the firm level. Similarly to the previous model, we also include firm- and year-fixed effects to control for unobserved factors that could affect the investment amounts.

Lastly, we extend our analysis to the heterogeneous forms, where we perform several triple DiD analyses (difference-in-difference-in-difference (DDD)). This allows us to observe how the policy change has affected firms with different characteristics, thus informing us of potential strategies that mediate or make the effect more pronounced.

In this case, for each specific heterogeneous group dummy that we will use individually created heterogeneous groups (hetergroup), where hetergroup = 1 or = 0 otherwise. We will use the following specification (6.3):

$$\ln\_outcome_{it} = \delta hetergroup * interaction_{it} + X_{it} + \alpha_i + \alpha_t + \epsilon_{it} \tag{6.3}$$

where our interaction dummy (interaction) further interacts with the heterogeneous group (hetergroup), we are concerned with, such as firm size, having green employees, paying environmental taxes, using subsidies in a dummy form, etc. All other variables remain the same.

6.4 Main results: The effect of the EI tax-credit phase-out

Table 6.4 provides coefficient estimates from specification (6.1) about each of the five primary outcomes: aggregated investment in cleaner production technologies (ln_netCP), investment into cleaner production technologies targeted at air-pollution reduction (ln_netCPair), investment into cleaner production technologies aimed at energy consumption reduction (ln_netCPenc), aggregated investment in end-of-pipe technologies (ln_netEP), and investment into end-of-pipe technologies directed at air-pollution reduction (ln_netEPair). Unless otherwise noted, all standard errors in this table and throughout the

Table 6.4 Main results—Difference-in-differences for adoption of green technologies

	ln_netCP	*ln_netCPair*	*ln_netCPenc*	*ln_netEP*	*ln_netEPair*
	(1)	(2)	(3)	(4)	(5)
Interaction	−2.03**	−2.35**	−3.31***	−0.73	−2.14**
	(0.78)	(1.03)	(1.11)	(1.13)	(1.02)
Controls	×	×	×	×	×
Firm FE	×	×	×	×	×
Year FE	×	×	×	×	×
R squared	0.01	0.00	0.01	0.01	0.04
N	1,413	1,276	1,197	1,194	1,277

Notes: Each coefficient is estimated from a separate regression following the main specification. Additional controls are firm size, sector, and year dummies, as well as green employees, environmental certifications, and lagged investment. Standard errors (in parentheses) are clustered at the firm level. *** $p < 0.01$, ** $p < 0.05$, and * $p < 0.1$.

Table 6.5 Main results—Event study of cleaner production technologies

	ln_netCP (1)	*ln_netCPair* (2)	*ln_netCPenc* (3)
Interaction ## 2011	−0.50	−0.76	−0.94
	(1.28)	(1.56)	(1.92)
Interaction ## 2012	−1.89	−0.73	−1.89
	(1.33)	(1.65)	(2.18)
Interaction ## 2013	−0.32	1.52	−1.44
	(1.32)	(1.75)	(2.46)
Interaction ## 2014	−0.30	0.63	−2.29
	(1.25)	(1.83)	(2.14)
Interaction ## 2015	−2.52*	−1.72	−4.63**
	(1.47)	(1.78)	(2.16)
Interaction ## 2016	−3.27**	−3.04	−4.70**
	(1.35)	(1.84)	(1.89)
Interaction ## 2017	−2.88**	−2.83	−5.83***
	(1.42)	(1.90)	(1.96)
Interaction ## 2018	−2.71*	−1.83	−4.38***
	(1.42)	(1.82)	(2.11)
Interaction ## 2019	−1.03	−1.48	−4.41*
	(1.40)	(1.88)	(2.30)
Interaction ## 2020	−2.97**	−2.52	−3.01
	(1.39)	(1.85)	(2.02)
Controls	×	×	×
Firm FE	×	×	×
Year FE	×	×	×
R-squared	0.01	0.00	0.00
N	1,413	1,276	1,197

Notes: Each coefficient is estimated from a separate regression following the main specification. Additional controls include firm size, sector, and year dummies, green employees, environmental certifications, and lagged investment. Standard errors (in parentheses) are clustered at the firm level. *** $p < 0.01$, ** $p < 0.05$, and * $p < 0.1$.

paper are clustered at the firm level. The findings suggest a negative impact of the tax-credit phase-out on investment in green technologies. Notably, this effect is more pronounced for CP technologies (−2.03), particularly those focused on reducing energy consumption (energy-efficient, −3.31), compared to EP technologies. However, given that the parallel-trends assumption does not hold for EP technologies, we cannot use the coefficient for interpretation. Thus, the evidence supports Hypothesis 1 and Hypothesis 2.

To gain further insights into the ramifications of the EI tax-credit phase-out, Tables 6.5 and 6.6 present the results from specification (6.2) for CP technologies and EP technologies, respectively. The results for CP technologies reveal that, before 2015, there were no significant differences in investment levels between the treatment and control groups. However, since

Table 6.6 Main results—Event study of end-of-pipe technologies

	ln_netEP (1)	*ln_netEPair* (2)
Interaction ## 2011	1.16	2.82
	(1.45)	(1.88)
Interaction ## 2012	3.79	2.38
	(1.54)	(1.75)
Interaction ## 2013	–0.15	4.01*
	(1.70)	(2.14)
Interaction ## 2014	–0.57	0.06
	(1.77)	(1.80)
Interaction ## 2015	–0.95	–0.87
	(1.62)	(1.54)
Interaction ## 2016	0.20	1.52
	(1.79)	(1.69)
Interaction ## 2017	–0.96	0.04
	(1.69)	(1.73)
Interaction ## 2018	–0.14	0.05
	(1.88)	(1.80)
Interaction ## 2019	1.18	–0.70
	(1.95)	(1.75)
Interaction ## 2020	1.25	–2.45
	(1.86)	(1.83)
Controls	×	×
Firm FE	×	×
Year FE	×	×
R-squared	0.06	0.10
N	1,227	1,194

Notes: Each coefficient is estimated from a separate regression following the main specification. Additional controls include firm size, sector, and year dummies, green employees, environmental certifications, and lagged investment. Standard errors (in parentheses) are clustered at the firm level. *** $p < 0.01$, ** $p < 0.05$, and * $p < 0.1$.

2015, investment has substantially declined, both at the aggregate level and specifically for energy-efficient technologies (ln_netCPenc). In contrast, we observe no discernible differences in investment levels before or after 2015 for aggregated EP technologies. Remarkably, for EP technologies targeted at air-pollution reduction (e.g., filters and sulphur scrubbers), there was a significant uptick in investment in 2013, indicating a strategic response by firms to the impending phase-out of the tax credit. Post-2015, the coefficients on policy phase-out are not statistically significant, suggesting that the phase-out primarily led to a reduction in investment in superior CP technologies rather than EP technologies; thus, further evidence also supports Hypothesis

1 and Hypothesis 2. In the subsequent section, these findings undergo empirical scrutiny through robustness tests, and an exploration of heterogeneous effects.

6.5 Robustness checks and extensions

Tables 6.7–6.13 present various extensions and robustness checks conducted during this study. These additional analyses aim to fortify the

Table 6.7 Robustness—Environmental R&D as dependent variable

	ln_RD (1)	*ln_RD* (2)
Interaction ## 2011	0.29 (0.68)	
Interaction ## 2012	0.80 (0.60)	
Interaction ## 2013	0.22 (0.60)	
Interaction ## 2014	0.82 (0.83)	
Interaction ## 2015	1.83** (0.79)	
Interaction ## 2016	1.40* (0.77)	
Interaction ## 2017	1.65* (0.90)	
Interaction ## 2018	1.66** (0.80)	
Interaction ## 2019	1.30* (0.70)	
Interaction ## 2020	1.08 (0.92)	
Interaction		1.08** (0.45)
Controls	×	×
Firm FE	×	×
Year FE	×	×
R-squared	0.06	0.22
N	1,227	1,514

Notes: Each coefficient is estimated from a separate regression following the main specification. Additional controls include firm size, sector, and year dummies, green employees, environmental certifications, and lagged investment. Standard errors (in parentheses) are clustered at the firm level. *** $p < 0.01$, ** $p < 0.05$, and * $p < 0.1$.

Table 6.8 Extensions—Heterogeneity with respect to size

	ln_netCP	*ln_netCPair*	*ln_netCPenc*	*ln_netEP*	*ln_netEPair*
	(1)	(2)	(3)	(4)	(5)
Interaction ##	−1.96**	−3.89***	0.57	−3.09***	−4.42***
big_firms	(0.80)	(1.14)	(1.14)	(1.18)	(1.10)
Controls	×	×	×	×	×
Firm FE	×	×	×	×	×
Year FE	×	×	×	×	×
R-squared	0.01	0.00	0.02	0.02	0.03
N	1,413	1,276	1,197	1,277	1,194
Interaction ##	−0.16	−1.74	1.92	−1.97	−2.06
medium_firms	(0.94)	(1.53)	(1.59)	(1.57)	(1.53)
Controls	×	×	×	×	×
Firm FE	×	×	×	×	×
Year FE	×	×	×	×	×
R-squared	0.02	0.00	0.02	0.02	0.03
N	1,413	1,276	1,197	1,277	1,194
Interaction ##	−4.78**	−1.42	2.04	1.51	1.67
small_firms	(2.23)	(2.03)	(1.65)	(2.22)	(1.38)
Controls	×	×	×	×	×
Firm FE	×	×	×	×	×
Year FE	×	×	×	×	×
R-squared	0.02	0.00	0.02	0.01	0.03
N	1,413	1,276	1,197	1,277	1,194

Notes: Each coefficient is estimated from a separate regression following the main specification. Additional controls include firm size, sector, and year dummies, green employees, environmental certifications, and lagged investment. Standard errors (in parentheses) are clustered at the firm level. *** $p < 0.01$, ** $p < 0.05$, and * $p < 0.1$.

reliability and comprehensiveness of our findings, offering a nuanced exploration of the dynamics surrounding the elimination of the EI tax credit and its repercussions on firms' behaviour. We provide evidence for a positive spillover on environmental R&D and present heterogeneous analysis regarding size. We study potential pathways for mediation of the negative investment shock of the EI tax-credit phase-out, such as green employees, subsidies, and environmental taxation. Finally, we provide a robustness check on bigger sample sizes and different definitions of the treatment and controls.

6.5.1 *Positive spillover on environmental R&D*

In the next section, we explored whether the phase-out of the EI tax credit had unintended consequences, particularly on environmental R&D, which also works as a robustness check. Table 6.7 details the outcomes from

Table 6.9 Extensions—Heterogeneity with respect to paying environmental taxation

	ln_netCP (1)	*ln_netCPair* (2)	*ln_netCPenc* (3)	*ln_netEP* (4)	*ln_netEPair* (5)
Tax in general					
Interaction	0.75	3.35**	−0.27	0.47	−0.66
	(0.85)	(1.34)	(1.40)	(1.56)	(1.53)
Controls	×	×	×	×	×
Firm FE	×	×	×	×	×
Year FE	×	×	×	×	×
R-squared	0.00	0.00	0.02	0.02	0.04
N	1,413	1,276	1,197	1,227	1,194
Large tax					
Interaction	−0.42	0.69	−2.27*	1.65	2.16
	(1.28)	(1.60)	(1.43)	(1.96)	(1.96)
Controls	×	×	×	×	×
Firm FE	×	×	×	×	×
Year FE	×	×	×	×	×
R-squared	0.02	0.00	0.03	0.03	0.06
N	1,413	1,276	1,197	1,227	1,194
Small tax					
Interaction	−0.31	0.93	1.54	−0.62	−1.96
	(1.34)	(2.05)	(1.79)	(1.82)	(1.76)
Controls	×	×	×	×	×
Firm FE	×	×	×	×	×
Year FE	×	×	×	×	×
R-squared	0.01	0.00	0.02	0.01	0.03
N	1,413	1,276	1,197	1,227	1,194

Notes: Each coefficient is estimated from a separate regression following the main specification. Additional controls include firm size, sector, and year dummies, green employees, environmental certifications, and lagged investment. Standard errors (in parentheses) are clustered at the firm level. *** $p < 0.01$, ** $p < 0.05$, and * $p < 0.1$.

Table 6.10 Extensions—Heterogeneity with respect to receiving subsidy

	ln_netCP (1)	*ln_netCPair* (2)	*ln_netCPenc* (3)	*ln_netEP* (4)	*ln_netEPair* (5)
Interaction ## subsidy	−1.24	−5.00***	1.03	−0.18	Omitted
	(1.67)	(1.73)	(2.29)	(2.25)	
Controls	×	×	×	×	×
Firm FE	×	×	×	×	×
Year FE	×	×	×	×	×
R-squared	0.01	0.00	0.03	0.02	Omitted
N	1,413	1,276	1,197	1,277	Omitted

Notes: Each coefficient is estimated from a separate regression following the main specification. Additional controls include firm size, sector, and year dummies, green employees, environmental certifications, and lagged investment. Standard errors (in parentheses) are clustered at the firm level. *** $p < 0.01$, ** $p < 0.05$, and * $p < 0$.

Table 6.11 Extensions—Heterogeneity with respect to having green employees

	ln_netCP (1)	*ln_netCPair* (2)	*ln_netCPenc* (3)	*ln_netEP* (4)	*ln_netEPair* (5)
Interaction ## subsidy	9.12**	0.12	−0.55	−2.32	−1.80
	(4.09)	(3.27)	(2.90)	(2.73)	(2.22)
Controls	×	×	×	×	×
Firm FE	×	×	×	×	×
Year FE	×	×	×	×	×
R-squared	0.01	0.00	0.02	0.02	0.03
N	1,413	1,276	1,197	1,277	1,194

Notes: Each coefficient is estimated from a separate regression following the main specification. Additional controls include firm size, sector, and year dummies, green employees, environmental certifications, and lagged investment. Standard errors (in parentheses) are clustered at the firm level. *** p < 0.01, ** p < 0.05, and * p < 0.1.

Table 6.12 Robustness—Only green technology adopters

	ln_netCP (1)	*ln_netCPair* (2)	*ln_netCPenc* (3)	*ln_netEP* (4)	*ln_netEPair* (5)
Interaction	−1.09**	−1.30**	−0.48	−0.84	−1.43***
	(0.44)	(0.55)	(0.60)	(0.59)	(0.52)
Controls	×	×	×	×	×
Firm FE	×	×	×	×	×
Year FE	×	×	×	×	×
R-squared	0.00	0.00	0.02	0.01	0.01
N	9,595	9,447	9,368	9,451	9,363

Notes: Each coefficient is estimated from a separate regression following the main specification. Additional controls include firm size, sector, and year dummies, green employees, environmental certifications, and lagged investment. Standard errors (in parentheses) are clustered at the firm level. *** p < 0.01, ** p < 0.05, and * p < 0.1.

Table 6.13 Robustness—Different definition of treatment and control

	ln_netCP (1)	*ln_netCPair* (2)	*ln_netCPenc* (3)	*ln_netEP* (4)	*ln_netEPair* (5)
Interaction	−2.51***	−1.91***	−0.75*	−1.57***	−1.25***
	(0.43)	(0.38)	(0.01)	(0.46)	(0.34)
Controls	×	×	×	×	×
Firm FE	×	×	×	×	×
Year FE	×	×	×	×	×
R-squared	0.00	0.00	0.01	0.00	0.00
N	37,798	37,650	37,571	37,654	37,566

Notes: Each coefficient is estimated from a separate regression following the main specification. Additional controls include firm size, sector, and year dummies, green employees, environmental certifications, and lagged investment. Standard errors (in parentheses) are clustered at the firm level. *** p < 0.01, ** p < 0.05, and * p < 0.1.

specifications (6.1) and (6.2) regarding investment in R&D, measured in natural logarithm. We can observe parallel trends prior 2015 and in contrast to the direct impacts observed on technology adoption, the EI tax-credit phase-out yielded positive effects on R&D post-2015. In response to the cessation of tax credits, it appears that firms temporarily redirected their resources towards the development of new green technologies rather than their immediate adoption. However, it is crucial to note that this positive effect is transient, as indicated by the statistically significant coefficient on the interaction term with 2019, albeit at the 10% significance level, and the lack of statistical significance for the coefficient in 2020. Additionally, the magnitude of these coefficients is smaller in comparison to the negative effects observed in Tables 6.4–6.6, as can be seen more clearly in Figure 6.6, thus confirming hypothesis 3. This shift in focus towards environmental R&D suggests an adaptive response by firms to the altered policy landscape, demonstrating a strategic reallocation of resources to innovate in green technology development rather than the immediate uptake of existing technologies.

6.5.2 *Heterogeneity with respect to size*

6.5.2.1 Extensions: Heterogeneity concerning size

The simple model presented in specification (6.1) illustrates that eliminating the EI tax credit has discernible effects on firms that were frequent users of the tax credit. It is plausible that additional firm-level characteristics influenced firms' responses to this policy alteration. Table 6.8 provides insights into the heterogeneity of results concerning firm size, where small firms have less employees than 50, medium firms 51–250, and large firms more than 250. The findings align with prior research (Tchorzewska, 2024), particularly highlighting the importance of the EI tax credit for small firms in facilitating financing for investments in superior CP technologies. This is evidenced by a notably large and negatively significant coefficient on ln_netCP, while no statistically significant coefficients are observed for the adoption of inferior EP technologies among small firms. Conversely, no statistically significant results are observed for medium-sized firms, while large firms experience a reduction in investment amounts in both CP and EP technologies. However, akin to the results presented in Tables 6.4–6.6, the negative coefficients in columns (4) and (5) for large firms are contingent on positive coefficients on investment into EP technologies during the years 2011–2014, indicative of a strategic response to the announcement of the EI tax-credit elimination. Given that this particular EI tax was intended to support majorly CP technologies, it seems smallest firms are the biggest losers of this tax-credit elimination.

This exploration of heterogeneity based on firm size underscores the varied impact of the EI tax-credit elimination on firms of different sizes. Small firms, heavily reliant on the tax credit for financing CP technologies, experience a more pronounced negative effect. In contrast, large firms exhibit a decline in investment across CP and EP technologies, with strategic adjustments evident in their pre-elimination investment patterns.

6.5.3 Mediating effects of the EI tax-credit elimination

6.5.3.1 Extensions: Heterogeneity concerning environmental taxation

Building upon the insights from the study by Tchórzewska et al. (2022) and Tchorzewska et al. (2025), we extended our investigation to explore whether firms that frequently utilise tax credits respond differently to the elimination of such credits, depending on their exposure to environmental taxation (Table 6.9). Our findings reveal interesting dynamics in alignment with previous literature, which underscores the synergistic effects of small environmental taxes with public financing. It would appear that when firms are subject to some form of environmental tax, the adverse effects of the EI tax-credit phase-out are largely mitigated, evident in the non-statistically significant coefficients. Moreover, for superior, CP technologies, the payment of an environmental tax not only nullifies the negative impact but also leads to an increase in investment levels post-phase-out. Additionally, the magnitude of the environmental taxation level paid emerges as a significant factor. While a modest level of environmental taxation effectively nullifies the negative effects of tax-credit phase-out, larger amounts fail to eliminate the decrease in investment in energy-efficient technologies—thus still leading to a drop in green technology adoption (ln_netCPenc). These findings underscore the interplay between environmental taxation and the consequences of tax-credit phase-outs. Firms subject to environmental taxes exhibit resilience against the negative effects of tax-credit elimination, with the level of taxation playing a crucial role in shaping their investment behaviour.

6.5.3.2 Extensions: Heterogeneity with respect to subsidy

In the subsequent analysis, we delved into whether receiving subsidies mediated the impact of the EI tax-credit phase-out. As presented in Table 6.10, the outcomes reveal that receiving subsidies indeed had a mediating effect. Specifically, our results indicate that receiving subsidies played a mediating role for both aggregated CP technologies and energy-efficient technologies (ln_netCPenc). However, this mediating effect was not observed for CP technologies specifically aimed at air-pollution reduction. This shows that frequent

EI tax-credit recipients when faced with a tax-credit elimination look for other sources of financing to sustain investment in CP technologies, or possibly cannot find any external sources of funding that could boost those investments.

6.5.3.3 Extensions: Heterogeneity concerning green employees

Interestingly, in the conclusive analysis presented in Table 6.11, it becomes evident that the presence of green employees serves as a successful mediator for the negative impact of the EI tax-credit elimination. For aggregated cleaner production, the coefficient is positive and statistically significant, demonstrating a substantial and positive effect. This suggests that having green employees mitigates the adverse effects of policy changes and contributes positively to investment decisions, despite a negative shock in place.

These findings imply that firms equipped with a workforce knowledgeable in green practices are better prepared to navigate policy alterations and display an increased propensity to invest in CP technologies (Demirel & Kesidou, 2019). This underlines the strategic value of fostering a workforce with environmental expertise, positioning firms to weather policy changes effectively and capitalise on opportunities for sustainable and environmentally conscious investments.

6.5.4 Sensitivity analysis

6.5.4.1 Robustness: Only green technology adopters

We have also performed the analysis on a bigger dataset, with a different definition of the treatment and control, but with a restriction that all firms must be green technology adopters, thus we are studying here the intensive margin rather than extensive margin of the EI tax-credit elimination. The resulting database has around 9,500 firm–year observations. Table 6.12 presents the results from the regressions. Similarly to the main results, we can observe negative and statistically significant coefficients on CP technologies (aggregated and aimed at air-pollution reduction); we can also observe negative coefficients on EP technologies and air-pollution–reducing technologies, but similarly as in the main results, this is driven by lack of parallel trends and excessive positive investment into EP technologies prior to 2015, rather than the effect of the EI tax-credit phase-out.

6.5.4.2 Robustness: Different definition of treatment and control groups

Lastly, we have also performed the analysis with a different definition of treatment and control groups (Table 6.13). In this case, we use a full subset of firms (around 37,600 observations); treatment is still observed more than once, while in the control group, we have both firms that received tax credit once and none at all. Our model specifications still have negative coefficients (1)–(5). It is important to note here, however, that because of the definition of our treatment and control, we no longer observe parallel trends. Thus, the coefficients here cannot be interpreted as the DiD estimates but rather as a fixed-effects panel regression with an interaction term.

6.6 Conclusions and policy recommendations

This study investigates the adaptive strategies firms employ in response to eliminating an environmental investment tax credit and explores the consequential impact on their innovativeness. We contribute to the existing literature on eco-innovation, environmental policies, and firm strategies by investigating the behavioural responses of a phase-out of an environmental investment tax credit, especially in the context of process eco-innovation.

Prior research has predominantly focused on the positive influence of subsidies on eco-innovation and has explored the crowding-out effects that subsidies (mostly R&D) typically entail. However, scant empirical attention has been paid to how firms react to modifications in mature subsidies and investment tax credits, especially their complete elimination (Matos et al., 2022). To our knowledge, this is the first paper to explore the removal of the EI tax credit from the Spanish Corporate Income Tax within the context of green technology adoption among manufacturing firms in Spain. We link these findings with broader environmental policy considerations.

Our analysis investigates firms' behavioural responses to the 2015 phase-out of the EI tax credit. The results reveal that, on a general scale, firms heavily reliant on tax credits have significantly curtailed their investments in superior CP technologies while not exhibiting a similar reduction in inferior EP technologies. Interestingly, in response to eliminating the EI tax credit, these same firms have intensified their investments in environmental R&D. This suggests a flexible reallocation of capital from one green technology objective to another, underscoring adaptability in response to policy changes, which can be a source of sustainable competitive advantage (Combs et al., 2011; Tuominen et al., 2004). Notably, this trend is more pronounced among small and large firms, with the smallest firms being particularly impacted by investment into superior CP technologies, making them the biggest losers.

Furthermore, we explore diverse strategies to mitigate the negative repercussions of EI tax-credit elimination. Our findings indicate that firms can shield themselves from the phase-out shock in various ways. Firstly, there are mediating effects on green technology adoption for firms that actively hire green employees. Secondly, using subsidies, thereby identifying alternative funding sources, proves effective in mediating the shock of EI tax-credit elimination. Lastly, regulators can play a role by introducing environmental taxes at a low level, serving as a mitigating factor against the negative shock associated with the elimination of EI tax credits. Indeed, it appears that as the "carrot" (EI tax credit) runs out, the "stick" (environmental tax) keeps the firms investing in green technologies.

Despite these insights, we must acknowledge certain limitations in our study. Eligibility criteria for tax credits are typically preferred in the evaluation context. However, we addressed this concern by focusing on the intensity of treatment. The announcement of the elimination of the EI tax credit in 2011 poses challenges in controlling for adaptation effects over time, despite efforts to address this through pre-2015 trend analysis. Additionally, the study's reliance on relatively modest sample size may impact the generalisability of results, although robustness checks indicate consistency across larger samples and varied definitions of control and treated groups. Future research avenues may involve exploring firm productivity indicators and pollution outcomes of firms resulting from this policy change. Addressing these limitations will provide a more comprehensive interpretation of our findings and serve as a foundation for further study.

In conclusion, the policy implications derived from our results underscore the need for careful consideration in green technology policy changes, as eliminating EI tax credits can have enduring negative impacts, which is undesirable during the times of green transition. However, if such phase-outs are inevitable, regulators might promote and encourage increasing green employment, as well as provide subsidies as alternatives or introduce low-level environmental taxes to sustain the level of green investment among frequent tax-credit recipients upon tax-credit's elimination.

7 Conclusions

7.1 What this book settles

This monograph has developed a view of green fiscal instruments operating as policy architectures that evolve over time. They are introduced into markets that already contain many regulations, standards—what researchers describe as a policy "mess" rather than a policy-mix (Greco et al., 2022), which make them difficult to evaluate. They also affect firms differently depending on their inherent characteristics, for example, size, profitability, access to finance, managerial capacity, or existing production technologies.

As argued in the Introduction, public debate often compresses these complexities into simplified moral categories. Carbon taxes become framed as either salvation or tyranny, while subsidies are portrayed as either industrial renaissance or rent-seeking theatre. This monograph treats green fiscal instruments as administrative technologies—imperfect tools intended to address double externality problem (Rennings, 2000) under constraints. Norwid's quote about sobriety in evaluation is central in this context. In the technical sense used throughout the book, sobriety refers to causal evaluation—the capacity to ask what a policy does in practice, how it changes investment and adoption, and whether it induces energy-efficient activity.

Two overarching conclusions emerge from this monograph. First, the empirical literature on the effectiveness of green fiscal policy in stimulating green technology adoption is expanding rapidly, yet, it remains methodologically uneven. As a result, the evidence is often insufficient to support strong causal claims; in many settings, findings are best interpreted as robust—though potentially confounded—correlations rather than identified causal effects. At the same time, the literature reviewed and empirical papers analysed support a reasonably confident characterisation of recurrent patterns, and it enables substantive engagement with the book's research questions, particularly those concerning instrument design, incentive intensity ("dose"), heterogeneity between cleaner-production and end-of-pipe technologies, policy-mixes under instrument intensity, and sequential effects of green fiscal policy. Looking forward, the "big data" era provides also grounds for cautious optimism.

DOI: 10.4324/9781003712398-7

Improved access to firm-level administrative data and policy-exposure measures, together with the growing feasibility of linking datasets across sources, should enable more credible causal inference on how green fiscal policies shape green technology adoption.

Second, the evidence and methodological synthesis indicate that policy effectiveness depends on instrument design and on the broader policy environment in which instruments operate. Incentives need to reach intensities that make adoption financially and operationally feasible by compensating for fixed costs, organisational disruption, and learning-by-doing during implementation. In addition, policy-mixes require coherence at a given point in time—in particular, an internally consistent "dose" across instruments—and credible sequencing over time. The evidence reviewed in this monograph suggests that sequences in which subsidies or tax credits are introduced first and then complemented by environmental taxation are more likely to shift investment towards energy-efficient and process-integrated technologies, because the initial support relaxes financing constraints while the subsequent price signal strengthens long-run incentives. By contrast, weak calibration or poorly coordinated overlap—such as an oversupply of subsidies and tax credits—can reduce marginal effectiveness and dilute behavioural responses.

The conclusions of this monograph rely on a precise definition of eco-innovation including both (i) process-integrated cleaner-production and energy-efficient technologies and (ii) compliance-oriented end-of-pipe abatement. Cleaner-production options typically require a drastic change of the production process, coordination across production lines and they often entail downtime, learning costs, managerial attention, and substantial fixed investment under uncertainty. End-of-pipe technologies may be indispensable for public health and short-run regulatory compliance, while less likely to change the underlying resource intensity of production.

7.2 Answers to research questions: Instrument effectiveness, dose, and redesign

The first set of research questions is concerned with the effectiveness of individual green fiscal instruments. Which instruments matter most for adoption, whether proportional increases in generosity translate into increased uptake, what minimum "dose" is required to trigger adoption, and whether instrument redesign can shift firms towards higher-impact technologies.

RQ1: Instrument effectiveness is conditional. Empirical evidence reviewed indicates that adoption responses depend on how an instrument's incentive profile—design, certainty, timing, and administrative burden—aligns with the barriers that firms face when adopting specific technologies (fixed costs, uncertainty, organisational disruption, and financing frictions). In the Spanish context, where environmental taxation is rather low and highly heterogeneous, they are generally associated with limited adoption responses and appear only more closely linked to energy-efficient technologies than to end-of-pipe. By contrast, subsidies and tax credits—measures that relax upfront capital constraints and shorten perceived payback horizons, which is especially problematic for smaller firms—tend to align more strongly with process-integrated upgrades, due to their design focused on energy efficiency in this setting.

RQ2–RQ3: Incentive intensity and non-linearity matter. The monograph provides consistent empirical evidence that incentive intensity influences adoption, with particularly clear associations for cleaner-production technologies. In the Environmental Investment (EI) tax credit case, a 1% increase in the credit is associated with an increase in investment in energy-efficient technologies of 0.41%, while investment in cleaner-production technologies targeted at air-pollution reduction increases by 1.39%. These elasticities support the conclusion that increases in green fiscal support can translate into measurable green adoption responses.

The evidence also suggests that adoption responses frequently exhibit non-linearities. In many settings, low-intensity incentives fail to move firms across adoption thresholds created by fixed costs or uncertainty. Once incentives reach levels that materially alter expected returns or reduce financing barriers, uptake becomes more likely and may accelerate through learning and organisational commitment. In the Spanish evidence reviewed, low levels of environmental taxation show weak or negligible associations with adoption, while higher levels are associated with positive and economically meaningful effects.

Intensity calibration translates into policy trade-offs. Higher taxation rates can impose competitiveness pressures and may affect competitiveness. High subsidy and tax-credit intensities can raise concerns about fiscal efficiency, opportunistic takeup, and potential crowding-out. The overall policy implication concerns calibration. Intensities need to be large enough to pass adoption thresholds while remaining consistent with fiscal capacity and competitiveness concerns. In the Spanish context reviewed, an indicative benchmark for environmental taxation intensity appears to be around EUR 2,500 per year on average.

RQ4: Instrument redesign can be successful, with heterogeneous effects across firms. Green fiscal policy architectures evolve through introductions, modifications, and withdrawals. Evidence reviewed indicates that redesign can reduce public financing of lower-impact or compliance-driven investments (end-of-pipe technologies) and can reorient incentives towards energy-efficiency margins in specific firm groups. Responses appear concentrated among firms facing binding capital constraints. In the EI tax credit modification case, the strongest investment shifts towards energy-efficient technologies occur among small firms (e.g., below 50 employees), consistent with liquidity constraints and greater sensitivity to financing conditions.

7.3 Answers to research questions: Policy-mixes as architecture through time

The second set of research questions is concerned with policy-mixes. Whether green fiscal policy instruments act as complements or substitutes, what "doses" of policy-mixes are effective, and whether particular sequencing of instruments affects effectiveness more.

RQ1: Policy-mix effects depend on design and intensity; cleaner production responds more consistently than end-of-pipe. Empirical results based on fixed-effects models with interaction terms and categorical treatment matching indicate that mixes combining environmental taxes with subsidies or tax credits do not produce uniformly positive effects. The sign and significance vary. However, where positive effects arise, they appear more consistently for cleaner-production technologies than for end-of-pipe abatement. This pattern aligns with a mechanism in which combined instruments both relax financing constraints and provide a cost signal that strengthens expectations about future environmental costs, thereby supporting process-integrated energy-efficient upgrades.

RQ2: "Doses" of policy-mixes matter. As shown in this monograph, empirical evidence indicates that low levels of environmental taxation often do not generate measurable adoption responses when implemented in isolation. This makes the findings on policy intensity within mixes particularly informative. The low tax levels appear more likely to matter when combined with subsidies or tax credits for green technology adoption. In such configurations, the mix can induce stronger adoption than subsidies alone, especially for cleaner-production technologies and, more specifically, energy-efficiency upgrades. By contrast, effects for end-of-pipe technologies are weaker and more conditional. Overall, these results support the view that well-calibrated policy mixes can address double externality simultaneously.

RQ3: Sequencing shapes investment behaviour. The sequential effects of green fiscal policies are somewhat an empirical novelty (OECD, 2025b; Tchorzewska et al., 2025). However, the empirical evidence indicates that more lenient environmental policies help introducing more stringent policies later on. Hence, the sequence of the green fiscal policy matters for green technology uptake—especially of energy-efficient technologies. Introducing subsidies or tax credits before environmental taxes can raise cleaner-production technologies' adoption more reliably than the reverse sequence. The evidence also indicates that sequencing matters for the durability of technological change. Stable and predictable trajectories (repeated environmental taxation) support investment planning and capability building into energy-efficient technologies, while short-lived or rapidly reversed incentives can shift behaviour towards short-term compliance. Lastly, stacking multiple generous support instruments (in any order) over time can reduce cleaner-production adoption in some settings.

7.4 Phase-out of the Environmental Investment tax credit

This monograph's most direct novel empirical contribution concerns policy withdrawal—investigated in Chapter 6, the 2015 phase-out of Spain's Environmental Investment (EI) tax credit—and its consequences for firm-level green technology adoption. Phase-outs are informative because they reveal how dependent is the green technology adoption on policy support and firms' adjustment margins under weakening incentives. To this aim, I have used firm-level data between 2010 and 2020 from the Spanish Institute of Statistics and applied difference-in-difference methodology, extended to difference-in-difference-in-difference to study policy-mixes and heterogeneous responses.

Four conclusions emerge. First, withdrawal effects differ by technology type. The phase-out disproportionately reduces investment in process-integrated cleaner-production and energy-efficient technologies, while end-of-pipe abatement remains stable. Second, frequent tax-credit users adjust through reallocation. Environmental R&D increases after the phase-out, indicating substitution across green objectives. Third, the contraction in cleaner-production investment is strongest among the smallest firms. Fourth, policy mixes and firm organisational capabilities seem to mitigate the shock. Green hiring, access to alternative financing through subsidies, and the presence of low-level environmental taxes reduce the adverse green technology adoption response. These results support a view that phase-outs require explicit architecture, and otherwise can create persistent losses in adoption of energy-efficient technologies.

7.5 Methodological conclusions

A consistent methodological message of the monograph is that empirical conclusions depend on the institutional setting, credibility of counterfactuals, measurement of variables, and treatment definitions. Different designs recover different estimands and involve distinct trade-offs between internal validity, external validity, and feasibility.

Regression discontinuity designs (RDDs) offer the strongest internal validity when policies create sharp thresholds. But their scope is local, identifying effects around eligibility cut-offs, and external validity depends on whether that local margin generalises. In addition, threshold-based eligibility is not common for many green fiscal instruments governing technology adoption, which limits the applicability of RDD in this domain.

Difference-in-differences designs provide a widely applicable causal framework when a policy introduction, redesign, or phase-out generates quasi-exogenous timing variation. Credibility depends on the plausibility of parallel trends (or suitable alternatives) and explicit modelling of anticipation and dynamic effects. Heterogeneity analysis strengthens interpretation in settings where treatment effects differ across firms or technology types.

Instrumental-variable (IV) approaches can address endogeneity under strong assumptions. When instruments are both relevant and satisfy exclusion restrictions, IV offers high internal validity for a well-defined group of compliers. External validity can be limited because IV typically identifies a local average treatment effect. Interpretation benefits from heterogeneity analysis.

Matching-based and categorical treatment designs help address "dose" questions by comparing firms across intensity regimes while balancing observed covariates. Their primary vulnerability is selection on unobservables, especially time-varying unobserved characteristics. These designs can be strengthened when institutional features generate quasi-exogenous variation in exposure, such as regional discretion over environmental taxation in Spain.

Fixed-effects models remain a baseline workhorse. They account for time-invariant firm heterogeneity and common time shocks, and they provide a disciplined starting point for empirical analysis, providing generally robust correlations. Their limitations concern time-varying confounders, evolving policy endogeneity, and anticipation effects, particularly in multi-treatment settings. Combining fixed effects with quasi-experimental designs can increase credibility when suitable variation exists.

Policy-mix and sequential evaluations remain frontier challenges. Multi-treatment environments complicate attribution and raise the risk of interpreting simple co-occurrence as genuine complementarity. Complementarity analysis provides one useful test in this setting by examining whether the marginal effect of one instrument increases when another instrument is present and more stringent, thereby moving beyond additive specifications towards mechanism-relevant interaction effects. In practice, however, such analyses are often constrained by limited access to high-resolution, firm-level exposure measures across multiple instruments. Sequential analysis offers an additional step forward by distinguishing the effects of different policy orderings. When combined with fixed-effects models, it can account for time-invariant unobserved firm heterogeneity and help organise the evidence around timing and adjustment. At the same time, sequential designs remain vulnerable to time-varying confounders, and self-selection into particular sequences, which means that causal interpretation still requires strong assumptions and, where possible, complementary identification strategies.

7.6 Limitations

The conclusions of this monograph are conditioned by recurring identification challenges in the empirical evaluation of green fiscal policy. Policy endogeneity remains a central threat because instruments may be introduced in sectors or regions already on a transition path, or in response to shocks—energy prices, competitiveness pressures, macroeconomic cycles—that influence adoption decisions directly. Anticipation and dynamic adjustment can affect estimates when firms accelerate, postpone, or reclassify investments around announced introductions, redesigns, or withdrawals, shifting observed timing without necessarily altering long-run behaviour. Multi-treatment settings generate attribution problems because overlapping instruments and concurrent regulatory changes can bias estimates when exposures and interaction structures are not modelled explicitly. Measurement limitations also constrain inference. Technology classifications may blur cleaner-production and end-of-pipe categories and adoption can be observed incompletely or with delay. External validity depends on institutional context, enforcement intensity, industrial structure, and financial conditions, which imply that extrapolation requires reasoning. Finally, the biggest limitation is access to data itself. Confidentiality and fragmented data ownership constrain the ability for the researchers to merge firm-level green technology adoption measures with precise multi-instrument exposure indicators, restricting the scope for the most demanding designs, particularly in sequential policy-mix evaluation.

7.7 Empirical evidence gaps

The monograph identifies several priorities for future research. A number of modern empirical approaches remain underused in the evaluation of green fiscal policy and green technology adoption, partly because they require institutional features and available granular data. These include regression discontinuity designs, complementarity analyses, and difference-in-differences studies that explicitly incorporate revenue recycling mechanisms.

Sequential policy-mix evaluation remains an active methodological frontier. Stronger evidence requires variation in instrument timing that can be treated as quasi-exogenous while holding other policy dimensions stable. In practice, this often implies multi-country firm-level data that provide rich variation in introductions, modifications, and phase-outs.

A third and central gap concerns productivity and competitiveness. Cleaner-production and energy-efficiency technologies plausibly support competitiveness by lowering operating costs (energy, materials, and water) while reducing emissions. This creates a pathway for aligning the energy trilemma with firm performance. OECD (2025b) highlights the scarcity of ex-post firm-level evidence on the effects of green policy mixes—especially sequential mixes—on productivity-related outcomes, such as employment, revenue, tangible assets, and broader performance indicators. A key next step for the literature involves linking adoption and innovation outcomes to productivity and pollution measures using credible exposure data and designs capable of handling repeated treatment and dynamic adjustment.

Bibliography

Acemoglu, D., Aghion, P., Bursztyn, L., & Hemous, D. (2012). The environment and directed technical change. *American Economic Review*, *102*(1), 131–166.

Aghion, P., Dechezleprêtre, A., Hemous, D., Martin, R., & Van Reenen, J. (2016). Carbon taxes, path dependency, and directed technical change: Evidence from the auto industry. *Journal of Political Economy*, *124*(1), 1–51.

Aghion, P., Hepburn, C., Teytelboym, A., & Zenghelis, D. (2019). Path dependence, innovation and the economics of climate change. In R. Fouquet (Ed.), *Handbook on green growth* (pp. 65–98). Edward Elgar.

Aldieri, L., Carlucci, F., Cirà, A., Ioppolo, G., & Vinci, C. P. (2019). Is green innovation an opportunity or a threat to employment? An empirical analysis of three main industrialized areas: The USA, Japan and Europe. *Journal of Cleaner Production*, *214*, 758–766.

Aldy, J. E., & Pizer, W. A. (2015). The competitiveness impacts of climate change mitigation policies. *Journal of the Association of Environmental and Resource Economists*, *2*(4), 565–595.

Allcott, H. (2011). Social norms and energy conservation. *Journal of Public Economics*, *95*(9–10), 1082–1095.

Allcott, H., & Greenstone, M. (2012). Is there an energy efficiency gap? *Journal of Economic Perspectives*, *26*(1), 3–28.

Allcott, H., Mullainathan, S., & Taubinsky, D. (2014). Energy policy with externalities and internalities. *Journal of Public Economics*, *112*, 72–88.

Ang, G., Röttgers, D., & Burli, P. (2017). *The empirics of enabling investment and innovation in renewable energy* (OECD Working Paper No. 123). https://www.oecd.org/en/publications/the-empirics-of-enabling-investment-and-innovation-in-renewable-energy_67d221b8-en.html (accessed 12.01.2026).

Antimiani, A., Costantini, V., & Paglialunga, E. (2023). Fossil fuels subsidy removal and the EU carbon neutrality policy. *Energy Economics*, *119*, 106524.

Arguedas, C., & van Soest, D. P. (2009). On reducing the windfall profits in environmental subsidy programs. *Journal of Environmental Economics and Management*, *58*(2), 192–205.

Arranz, N., Arroyabe, M., Molina-García, A., & De Arroyabe, J. F. (2019). Incentives and inhibiting factors of eco-innovation in the Spanish firms. *Journal of Cleaner Production*, *220*, 167–176.

Arrow, K. J. (1962). The economic implications of learning by doing. *The Review of Economic Studies*, *29*(3), 155–173.

Arzaghi, M., & Squalli, J. (2023). The environmental impact of fossil fuel subsidy policies. *Energy Economics*, *126*, 106980.

Autor, D. H. (2003). Outsourcing at will: The contribution of unjust dismissal doctrine to the growth of employment outsourcing. *Journal of Labor Economics*, *21*(1), 1–42.

Ayoub, M., & Lhuillery, S. (2024). Mix and match: What is the best R&D recipe for eco-innovation?. *Industry and Innovation*, *31*(7), 896–921.

Bai, Y., Song, S., Jiao, J., & Yang, R. (2019). The impacts of government R&D subsidies on green innovation: Evidence from Chinese energy-intensive firms. *Journal of Cleaner Production*, *233*, 819–829.

Baranzini, A., & Carattini, S. (2017). Effectiveness, earmarking and labeling: Testing the acceptability of carbon taxes with survey data. *Environmental Economics and Policy Studies*, *19*(1), 197–227.

Barreiro Carril, M. C. (2015). *Spanish tax credit for investments in environmental protection: An example of a tax incentive compatible with EU rules on state aid* (WU International Taxation Research Paper Series *2015-01*).

Bashmakov, I. A., Nilsson, L. J., Acquaye, A., Bataille, C., Cullen, J. M., de la, R., du Can, S., Fischedick, M., Geng, Y., & Tanaka, K. (2022). Industry. In P. R. Shukla, J. Skea, R. Slade, A. Al Khourdajie, R. van Diemen, D. McCollum, M. Pathak, S. Some, P. Vyas, R. Fradera, M. Belkacemi, A. Hasija, G. Lisboa, S. Luz, & J. Malley (Eds.), *Climate change 2022: Mitigation of climate change* (pp. 1161–1225). Cambridge University Press.

Baumol, W. J., & Oates, W. E. (1988). *The theory of environmental policy*. Cambridge University Press.

Bergek, A., & Jacobsson, S. (2010). Are tradable green certificates a cost-efficient policy driving technical change or a rent-generating machine? Lessons from Sweden 2003–2008. *Energy Policy*, *38*(3), 1255–1271.

Bergek, A., Jacobsson, S., Carlsson, B., Lindmark, S., & Rickne, A. (2008). Analyzing the functional dynamics of technological innovation systems: A scheme of analysis. *Research Policy*, *37*(3), 407–429.

Biggi, G., Mina, A., & Tamagni, F. (2023). There are different shades of green: Heterogeneous environmental innovations and their effects on firm performance. *arXiv preprint arXiv:2310.08353*.

Bloom, N., Genakos, C., Martin, R., & Sadun, R. (2010). Modern management: Good for the environment or just hot air? *The Economic Journal*, *120*(544), 551–572.

Böhringer, C., Garcia-Muros, X., & González-Eguino, M. (2019). Greener and fairer. *Economics of Energy & Environmental Policy*, *8*(2), 141–160.

Bossle, M. B., de Barcellos, M. D., Vieira, L. M., & Sauvée, L. (2016). The drivers for adoption of eco-innovation. *Journal of Cleaner Production*, *113*, 861–872.

Bronzini, R., & Iachini, E. (2014). Are incentives for R&D effective? Evidence from a regression discontinuity approach. *American Economic Journal: Economic Policy*, *6*(4), 100–134.

Buccella, D., Fanti, L., Gori, L., & Tchórzewska, K. B. (2025). Price-based emissions reduction policies in a polluting managerial duopoly. *Central European Management Journal*, *33*(4), 547–574.

Cai, W., & Li, G. (2018). The drivers of eco-innovation and its impact on performance: Evidence from China. *Journal of Cleaner Production*, *176*, 110–118.

Cainelli, G., De Marchi, V., & Grandinetti, R. (2015). Does the development of environmental innovation require different resources? Evidence from Spanish manufacturing firms. *Journal of Cleaner Production*, *94*, 211–220.

Cainelli, G., & Mazzanti, M. (2013). Environmental innovations in services: Manufacturing–services integration and policy transmissions. *Research Policy*, *42*(9), 1595–1604.

Capelle, M. D., Kirti, M. D., Pierri, M. N., & Bauer, M. G. V. (2023). *Mitigating climate change at the firm level: Mind the laggards*. International Monetary Fund.

Carattini, S., Carvalho, M., & Fankhauser, S. (2018). Overcoming public resistance to carbon taxes. *Wiley Interdisciplinary Reviews: Climate Change*, *9*(5), e531.

Carraro, C., De Cian, E., Nicita, L., Massetti, E., & Verdolini, E. et al (2010). Environmental policy and technical change: A survey. *International Review of Environmental and Resource Economics*, *4*(2), 163–219.

Carree, M., Lokshin, B., & Belderbos, R. (2011). A note on testing for complementarity and substitutability in the case of multiple practices. *Journal of Productivity Analysis*, *35*(3), 263–269.

Cecere, G., & Mazzanti, M. (2017). Green jobs and eco-innovations in European SMEs. *Resource and Energy Economics*, *49*, 86–98.

Cecere, G., Corrocher, N., & Mancusi, M. L. (2020). Financial constraints and public funding of eco-innovation: Empirical evidence from European SMEs. *Small Business Economics*, *54*(1), 285–302.

Chiappini, R., Montmartin, B., Pommet, S., & Demaria, S. (2022). Can direct innovation subsidies relax SMEs' financial constraints? *Research Policy*, *51*(5), 104493.

Chronopoulos, M., Hagspiel, V., & Fleten, S.-E. (2016). Stepwise green investment under policy uncertainty. *The Energy Journal*, *37*(4), 87–108.

Cingano, F., Palomba, G., Pinotti, P., & Rettore, E. (2023). The heterogeneous effects of firm subsidies. *Labour Economics*, *83*, Article 102390. https://doi.org/10.1016/j.labeco.2023.102390

Combs, J. G., Ketchen, D. J. Jr, Ireland, R. D., & Webb, J. W. (2011). The role of resource flexibility in leveraging strategic resources. *Journal of Management Studies*, *48*(5), 1098–1125.

Connolly, K., Allan, G. J., & McIntyre, S. G. (2016). The evolution of green jobs in Scotland: A hybrid approach. *Energy Policy*, *88*, 355–360. https://doi.org/10.1016/j.enpol.2015.10.044

Costantini, V., Crespi, F., & Palma, A. (2017). Characterizing the policy mix and its impact on eco-innovation: A patent analysis of energy-efficient technologies. *Research Policy*, *46*(4), 799–819.

Criscuolo, C., Martin, R., Overman, H. G., & Van Reenen, J. (2019). Some causal effects of an industrial policy. *American Economic Review*, *109*(1), 48–85.

Cuerva, M. C., Triguero-Cano, Á, & Córcoles, D. (2014). Drivers of green and non-green innovation: Empirical evidence in low-tech SMEs. *Journal of Cleaner Production*, *68*, 104–113.

Czarnitzki, D., & Hottenrott, H. (2011). Financial contraints: Routine versus cutting edge R&D investment. *Journal of Economics and Management Strategy*, *20*(1), 121–157.

Dabla-Norris, E., Khalid, S., Magistretti, G., & Sollaci, A. (2024). Does information change public support for climate mitigation policies? *Climate Policy*, *24*(10), 1474–1487.

Daugbjerg, C., & Kay, A. (2020). Policy feedback and pathways: When change leads to endurance and continuity to change. *Policy Sciences*, *53*(2), 253–268.

Dechezleprêtre, A., Einiö, E., Martin, R., Nguyen, K. T., & Van Reenen, J. (2023). Do tax incentives increase firm innovation? An RD design for R&D, patents, and spillovers. *American Economic Journal: Economic Policy*, *15*(4), 486–521.

Dechezleprêtre, A., Nachtigall, D., & Venmans, F. (2018). *The joint impact of the European union emissions trading system on carbon emissions and economic performance* (OECD Economics Department Working Papers, No. 1515). OECD Publishing.

Dechezleprêtre, A., & Sato, M. (2017). The impacts of environmental regulations on competitiveness. *Review of Environmental Economics and Policy*, 11(2), 183–206.

De Groote, O., & Verboven, F. (2019). Subsidies and time discounting in new technology adoption: Evidence from solar photovoltaic systems. *American Economic Review*, *109*(6), 2137–2172.

del Rio, P., & Burguillo, M. (2009). An empirical analysis of the impact of renewable energy deployment on local sustainability. *Renewable and Sustainable Energy Reviews*, *13*(6–7), 1314–1325.

del Rio, P., & Howlett, M. P. (2013). *Beyond the'Tinbergen rule'in policy design: Matching tools and goals in policy portfolios* (Lee Kuan Yew School of Public Policy Research Paper, No. 13–01). https://ssrn.com/abstract=2247238

del Río, P., García-Quevedo, J., & Martínez-Ros, E. (2021). La ecoinnovación en España: situación, determinantes y políticas. *Papeles de Economía Española*, (169), 150–164.

del Río, P., Peñasco, C., & Romero-Jordán, D. (2015). Analysing firm-specific and type-specific determinants of eco-innovation. *Environmental Innovation and Societal Transitions*, *17*, 69–95.

Del Río, P., Peñasco, C., & Romero-Jordán, D. (2016). What drives eco-innovators? A critical 533 review of the empirical literature based on econometric methods. *Journal of Cleaner Production*, *534*(112), 2158–2170.

Del Río, P., Romero-Jordán, D., & Peñasco, C. (2017). Analysing firm-specific and type-specific determinants of eco-innovation. *Technological and Economic Development of Economy*, *23*(2), 270–295.

De Marchi, V. (2012). Environmental innovation and R&D cooperation: Empirical evidence from 527 Spanish manufacturing firms. *Research Policy*, *41*(3), 614–623.

Demirel, P., & Kesidou, E. (2011). Stimulating different types of eco-innovation in the UK: Government policies and firm motivations. *Ecological Economics*, *70*(8), 1546–1557.

Demirel, P., & Kesidou, E. (2019). Sustainability-oriented capabilities for eco-innovation: Meeting the regulatory, technology, and market demands. *Business Strategy and the Environment*, *28*(5), 847–857.

Denes, M., Howell, S. T., Mezzanotti, F., Wang, X., & Xu, T. (2023). Investor tax credits and entrepreneurship: Evidence from us states. *The Journal of Finance*, *78*(5), 2621–2671.

Donis, S., Gómez, J., & Salazar, I. (2023). Economic complexity, property rights and the judicial system as drivers of eco-innovations: An analysis of OECD countries. *Technovation*, *128*, 102868.

Douenne, T., & Fabre, A. (2022). Yellow vests, pessimistic beliefs, and carbon tax aversion. *American Economic Journal: Economic Policy*, *14*(1), 81–110.

Energy Institute. (2024). Statistical review of world energy 2024 (73rd ed.). https://www.energyinst.org/__data/assets/pdf_file/0006/1542714/684_EI_Stat_Review_V16_DIGITAL.pdf

European Commission. (2022, May 18). *REPowerEU plan* (Communication from the Commission to the European Parliament, the European Council, the Council, the European Economic and Social Committee and the Committee of the Regions, COM/2022/230 final). EUR-Lex.

European Commission. (2025). Energy poverty. https://energy.ec.europa.eu/topics/markets-and-consumers/energy-consumers-and-prosumers/energy-poverty_en

Farrell, M. J. (1957). The measurement of productive efficiency. *Journal of the Royal Statistical Society Series A: Statistics in Society*, *120*(3), 253–281.

Feng, T., Ma, J., Yang, Y., & Mi, Z. (2025). Synergistic effects of air pollution control policies: Evidence from China. *Journal of Environmental Management*, *373*, 123581.

Fischer, C., & Newell, R. G. (2008). Environmental and technology policies for climate mitigation. *Journal of Environmental Economics and Management*, *55*(2), 142–162.

Flanagan, K., Uyarra, E., & Laranja, M. (2011). Reconceptualising the 'policy mix' for innovation. *Research Policy*, *40*(5), 702–713.

Fraser, I., & Hone, P. (2003). Agricultural land retirement: Lessons from an Australian case study. *Land Use Policy*, *20*(1), 61–72.

Frey, M., Iraldo, F., & Testa, F. (2013). The determinants of innovation in green supply chains: Evidence from an Italian sectoral study. *R&D Management*, *43*(4), 352–364.

Frondel, M., Horbach, J., & Rennings, K. (2007). End-of-pipe or cleaner production? An empirical 547 comparison of environmental innovation decisions across OECD countries. *Business Strategy and 548 Environment*, *16*(8), 571–584.

Fujiwara, N. (2006). The political economy of environmental taxation in European countries (CEPS Working Document No. 245). CEPS.

Fullerton, D., & Heutel, G. (2007). Who bears the burden of a tax on carbon emissions in Japan? *Environmental Economics and Policy Studies*, *8*(4), 255–270.

Gagliardi, L., Marin, G., & Miriello, C. (2016). The greener the better? Job creation effects of environmentally-friendly technological change. *Industrial and Corporate Change*, *25*(5), 779–807.

García-Piqueres, G., & García-Ramos, R. (2024). Environmental corporate social responsibility practices and firm innovation: Complementarities and empirical evidence from Spanish firms. *Heliyon*, *10*(8).

Garcia-Quevedo, J., & Jove-Llopis, E. (2021). Environmental policies and energy efficiency investments. An industry-level analysis. *Energy Policy*, *156*, 112461.

García-Quevedo, J., Martínez-Ros, E., & Tchorzewska, K. (2022). End-of-pipe and cleaner production technologies: Do they respond to different drivers? *Journal of Cleaner Production*, *340*, 130786.

Gelabert, L., Fosfuri, A., & Tribo, J. A. (2009). Does the effect of public support for R&D depend on the degree of appropriability? *The Journal of Industrial Economics*, *57*(4), 736–767.

Gerarden, T. D., Newell, R. G., & Stavins, R. N. (2017). Assessing the energy-efficiency gap. *Journal of Economic Literature*, *55*(4), 1486–1525.

Ghisetti, C., Mancinelli, S., Mazzanti, M., & Zoli, M. (2017). Financial barriers and environmental innovations: Evidence from EU manufacturing firms. *Climate Policy*, *17*(Suppl 1), S131–S147.

Ghisetti, C., & Rennings, K. (2014). Environmental innovations and profitability: How does it pay to be green? An empirical analysis on the German innovation survey. *Journal of Cleaner Production*, *75*, 106–117.

Gillingham, K., Newell, R. G., & Palmer, K. (2009). Energy efficiency economics and policy. *Annual Review of Resource Economics*, *1*(1), 597–620.

Gillingham, K., & Palmer, K. (2014). Bridging the energy efficiency gap: Policy insights from economic theory and empirical evidence. *Review of Environmental Economics and Policy*, *8*(1), 18–38.

Gonzales, L. E., Ito, K., & Reguant, M. (2023). The investment effects of market integration: Evidence from renewable energy expansion in Chile. *Econometrica*, *91*(5), 1659–1693.

Gonzalez, X., Jaumandreu, J., & Pazo, C. (2005). Barriers to innovation and subsidy effectiveness. *RAND Journal of Economics*, *36*(4), 930–950.

González, P. F., Presno, M. J., & Landajo, M. (2024). Tracking the change in Spanish greenhouse gas emissions through an LMDI decomposition model: A global and sectoral approach. *Journal of Environmental Sciences*, *139*, 114–122.

González, X., & Pazó, C. (2008). Do public subsidies stimulate private R&D spending? *Research Policy*, *37*(3), 371–389.

Goulder, L. H., & Parry, I. W. (2008). Instrument choice in environmental policy. *Review of Environmental Economics and Policy*, *2*(2) 152–174.

Goulder, L. H., & Schneider, S. H. (1999). Induced technological change and the attractiveness of CO_2 abatement policies. *Resource and Energy Economics*, *21*(3–4), 211–253.

Greco, M., Germani, F., Grimaldi, M., & Radicic, D. (2022). Policy mix or policy mess? Effects of cross-instrumental policy mix on eco-innovation in German firms. *Technovation*, *117*, 102194.

Griliches, Z. (1992). Introduction to "output measurement in the service sectors". In *Output measurement in the service sectors* (pp. 1–22). University of Chicago Press.

Guerzoni, M., & Raiteri, E. (2015). Demand-side vs. supply-side technology policies: Hidden treatment and new empirical evidence on the policy mix. *Research Policy*, *44*(3), 726–747.

Hagspiel, V., Nunes, C., Oliveira, C., & Portela, M. (2021). Green investment under time-dependent subsidy retraction risk. *Journal of Economic Dynamics and Control*, *126*, 103936.

Hall, B. H., Jaffe, A. B., & Trajtenberg, M. (2000). *Market value and patent citations: A first look*. https://www.nber.org/system/files/working_papers/w7741/w7741.pdf

Hall, R. E., & Jorgenson, D. W. (1967). Tax policy and investment behavior. *The American Economic Review*, *57*(3), 391–414.

Haller, S. A., & Murphy, L. (2012). Corporate expenditure on environmental protection. *Environ564 Mental and Resource Economics*, *51*(2), 277–296.

Hashemi, M., Jenkins, G., & Milne, F. (2024). Renewable energy support through feed-in tariffs: A retrospective stakeholder analysis. *Journal of Benefit-Cost Analysis*, *15*(2), 276–301.

Hassett, K. A., & Hubbard, R. G. (2002). Tax policy and business investment. In *Handbook of public economics* (Vol. 3, pp. 1293–1343). Elsevier.

Hassett, K. A., & Metcalf, G. E. (1993). Energy conservation investment: Do consumers discount the future correctly? *Energy Policy*, *21*(6), 710–716.

Hicks, J. R. (1932). Marginal productivity and the principle of variation. *Economica*, (35), 79–88.

Hojnik, J., & Ruzzier, M. (2016). What drives eco-innovation? A review of an emerging literature. *Environmental Innovation and Societal Transitions*, *19*, 31–41.

Horbach, J. (2008). Determinants of environmental innovation—New evidence from German panel 567 data sources. *Research Policy*, *37*(1), 163–173.

Horbach, J. (2016). Empirical determinants of eco-innovation in European countries using the Community Innovation Survey. *Environmental Innovation and Societal Transitions*, *19*, 1–14. https://doi.org/10.1016/j.eist.2015.09.005

Horbach, J. (2019). Determinants of eco-innovation at the firm level. *Handbook of sustainable innovation* (pp. 60–77). Edward Elgar Publishing.

Horbach, J., Oltra, V., & Belin, J. (2013). Determinants and specificities of eco-innovations compared to other innovations—An econometric analysis for the French and German industry based on the community innovation survey. *Industry and Innovation*, *20*(6), 523–543.

Horbach, J., Rammer, C., & Rennings, K. (2012). Determinants of eco-innovations by type of environmental impact—The role of regulatory push/pull, technology push and market pull. *Ecological Economics*, *78*, 112–122.

Horbach, J., & Rennings, K. (2013). Environmental innovation and employment dynamics in different technology fields–an analysis based on the German Community Innovation Survey 2009. *Journal of Cleaner Production*, *57*, 158–165.

Hötte, K. (2020). How to accelerate green technology diffusion? Directed technological change in the presence of coevolving absorptive capacity. *Energy Economics*, *85*, 104565.

Howlett, M. (2019). Procedural policy tools and the temporal dimensions of policy design. resilience, robustness and the sequencing of policy mixes. *International Review of Public Policy*, *1*(1), 27–45.

Hryckiewicz, A., Tchorzewska, K. B., Borsuk, M., & Tsomocos, D. P. (2023). *Navigating the digital frontier* (National Bank of Poland Working Paper No. 367). National Bank of Poland.

Hu, D., Qiu, L., She, M., & Wang, Y. (2021). Sustaining the sustainable development: How do firms turn government green subsidies into financial performance through green innovation. *Business Strategy and the Environment*, *30*(5), 2271–2292.

Immervoll, H. (2024). *Financing social protection in OECD countries: Role and uses of revenue earmarking* (SSRN working paper).

Immervoll, H., Linden, J., O'Donogue, C., & Sologon, D. M. (2023). *Who pays for higher carbon prices? Illustration for Lithuania and a research agenda* (IZA Discussion Papers No. 15868). IZA Institute of Labor Economics.

Intergovernmental Panel on Climate Change. (2005). *Carbon dioxide capture and storage: Technical summary (IPCC special report on carbon dioxide capture and storage)*. Cambridge University Press. https://archive.ipcc.ch/pdf/special-reports/srccs/srccs_technicalsummary.pdf

International Energy Agency (2023). Electricity grids and secure energy transitions. https://www.iea.org/reports/electricity-grids-and-secure-energy-transitions

International Energy Agency. (2024a). Global overview – Renewables 2024. https://www.iea.org/reports/renewables-2024/global-overview

International Energy Agency. (2024b). Electricity – Renewables 2024. https://www.iea.org/reports/renewables-2024/electricity

International Energy Agency. (2024c). *Electricity 2024: Analysis and forecast to 2026.* https://www.iea.org/reports/electricity-2024

International Energy Agency. (2024d). Energy efficiency 2024. https://www.iea.org/reports/energy-efficiency-2024

International Energy Agency. (2025a). Electricity 2025: Analysis and forecast to 2027. https://www.iea.org/reports/electricity-2025

International Energy Agency. (2025b). Global energy review 2025. https://www.iea.org/reports/global-energy-review-2025

International Energy Agency. (2025c). *Energy and AI*. https://www.iea.org/reports/energy-and-ai

International Energy Agency (2025d) *Global* critical minerals *Outlook 2025*. https://www.iea.org/reports/global-critical-minerals-outlook-2025

International Energy Agency. (2025e). Energy efficiency 2025. https://www.iea.org/reports/energy-efficiency-2025

International Organization for Standardization. (2018). ISO 50001:2018—Energy management systems—Requirements with guidance for use. https://www.iso.org/standard/69426.html

Jaffe, A. B., Newell, R. G., & Stavins, R. N. (2002). Environmental policy and technological change. *Environmental and Resource Economics*, *22*(1), 41–70.

Jaffe, A. B., Newell, R. G., & Stavins, R. N. (2003). Technological change and the environment. In *Handbook of environmental economics* (Vol. 1, pp. 461–516). Elsevier.

Jaffe, A. B., Newell, R. G., & Stavins, R. N. (2005). A tale of two market failures: Technology and environmental policy. *Ecological Economics*, *54*(2–3), 164–174.

Jaffe, A. B., & Palmer, K. (1997). Environmental regulation and innovation: A panel data study. *Review of Economics and Statistics*, *79*(4), 610–619.

Jaffe, A. B., & Stavins, R. N. (1994a). The energy paradox and the diffusion of conservation technology. *Resource and Energy Economics*, *16*(2), 91–122.

Jaffe, A. B., & Stavins, R. N. (1994b). The energy-efficiency gap what does it mean? *Energy Policy*, *22*(10), 804–810.

Jarvis, S. (2024). The economic costs of NIMBYism: Evidence from renewable energy projects. *Journal of the Association of Environmental and Resource Economists*. *12*(4), 983–1022.

Jia, Z., & Lin, B. (2021). The impact of removing cross subsidies in electric power industry in China: Welfare, economy, and CO_2 emission. *Energy Policy*, *148*, 111994.

Jové-Llopis, E., & Segarra-Blasco, A. (2018). Eco-innovation strategies: A panel data analysis of Spanish manufacturing firms. *Business Strategy and the Environment*, *27*(8), 1209–1220.

Kahneman, D., Knetsch, J. L., & Thaler, R. H. (1991). Anomalies: The endowment effect, loss aversion, and status quo bias. *Journal of Economic Perspectives*, *5*(1), 193–206.

Kemp, R., & Pontoglio, S. (2011). The innovation effects of environmental policy instruments—A typical case of the blind men and the elephant? *Ecological Economics*, *72*, 28–36.

Kerr, S., & Newell, R. G. (2003). Policy-induced technology adoption: Evidence from the US lead phasedown. *The Journal of Industrial Economics*, *51*(3), 317–343.

Kiefer, C. P., Del Río González, P., & Carrillo-Hermosilla, J. (2019). Drivers and barriers of eco-innovation types for sustainable transitions: A quantitative perspective. *Business Strategy and the Environment*, *28*(1), 155–172.

Klenert, D., Mattauch, L., Combet, E., Edenhofer, O., Hepburn, C., Rafaty, R., & Stern, N. (2018). Making carbon pricing work for citizens. *Nature Climate Change*, *8*(8), 669–677.

Kozlova, M., Huhta, K., & Lohrmann, A. (2023). The interface between support schemes for renewable energy and security of supply: Reviewing capacity mechanisms and support schemes for renewable energy in Europe. *Energy Policy*, *181*, 113707.

Laibson, D. (1997). Golden eggs and hyperbolic discounting. *The Quarterly Journal of Economics*, *112*(2), 443–478.

Lehmann, P., & Gawel, E. (2013). Why should support schemes for renewable electricity complement the EU emissions trading scheme? *Energy Policy*, *52*, 597–607.

Leipprand, A., Flachsland, C., & Pahle, M. (2020). Starting low, reaching high? Sequencing in EU climate and energy policies. *Environmental Innovation and Societal Transitions*, *37*, 140–155.

Lenihan, H., Mulligan, K., Perez-Alaniz, M., & Rammer, C. (2025a). R&D policy instrument mix sequencing: Evaluating the impact of receiving R&D grants and R&D tax credits over time on firm-level R&D. *Industry and Innovation*, *32*(5), 540–573.

Lenihan, H., Mulligan, K., Perez-Alaniz, M., & Rammer, C. (2025b). Serving the right menu of R&D policy instruments to firms: An analysis of policy mix sequencing. *Annual Review of Policy Design*, *13*. https://ojs.unbc.ca/index.php/design/article/view/2075

Lerche, A. (2025). Direct and indirect effects of investment tax incentives. *American Economic Review*, *115*(8), 2781–2818.

Li, M., Cao, G., Cui, L., Liu, X., & Dai, J. (2023). Examining how government subsidies influence firms' circular supply chain management: The role of eco-innovation and top management team. *International Journal of Production Economics*, *261*, 108893.

Li, Z., Zheng, C., Liu, A., Yang, Y., & Yuan, X. (2022). Environmental taxes, green subsidies, and cleaner production willingness: Evidence from China's publicly traded companies. *Technological Forecasting and Social Change*, *183*, 121906.

Lilliestam, J., Patt, A., & Bersalli, G. (2021). The effect of carbon pricing on technological change for full energy decarbonization: A review of empirical ex-post evidence. *Wiley Interdisciplinary Reviews: Climate Change*, *12*(1), e681.

Long, S., & Liao, Z. (2021). Are fiscal policy incentives effective in stimulating firms' eco-product innovation? The moderating role of dynamic capabilities. *Business Strategy and the Environment*, *30*(7), 3095–3104.

Lüthi, S., & Wüstenhagen, R. (2012). The price of policy risk—Empirical insights from choice experiments with European photovoltaic project developers. *Energy Economics*, *34*(4), 1001–1011.

Ma, C., & Peng, D. (2025). Government subsidies, environmental costs, and green innovation. *International Review of Economics & Finance*, *101*, 104237.

Ma, Y., Sha, Y., Wang, Z., & Zhang, W. (2023). The effect of the policy mix of green credit and government subsidy on environmental innovation. *Energy Economics*, *118*, 106512.

Maestre-Andrés, S., Drews, S., & Van Den Bergh, J. (2019). Perceived fairness and public acceptability of carbon pricing: A review of the literature. *Climate Policy*, *19*(9), 1186–1204.

Marino, M., Lhuillery, S., Parrotta, P., & Sala, D. (2016). Additionality or crowding-out? An overall evaluation of public R&D subsidy on private R&D expenditure. *Research Policy*, *45*(9), 1715–1730.

Marino, M., Parrotta, P., Tchorzewska, K., & Appio, F. (2024). *Larger subsidies, greener technologies? Assessing the influence of environmental funding on the Dutch manufacturing firms* (working paper).

Martin, R., De Preux, L. B., & Wagner, U. J. (2014). The impact of a carbon tax on manufacturing: Evidence from microdata. *Journal of Public Economics*, *117*, 1–14.

Martínez-Ros, E., & Kunapatarawong, R. (2019). Green innovation and knowledge: The role of size. *Business Strategy and the Environment*, *28*(6), 1045–1059.

Mas-Colell, A., Whinston, M. D., & Green, J. R. (1995). *Microeconomic theory* (Vol. 1). Oxford University Press.

Massetti, E., & Bellon, M. M. (2022). *Planning and mainstreaming adaptation to climate change in fiscal policy*. International Monetary Fund.

Matos, S., Viardot, E., Sovacool, B. K., Geels, F. W., & Xiong, Y. (2022). Innovation and climate change: A review and introduction to the special issue. *Technovation*, *117*, 102612.

Mazzanti, M., & Zoboli, R. (2008). Complementarities, firm strategies and environmental innovations: Empirical evidence for a district based manufacturing system. *Environmental Sciences*, *5*(1), 17–40.

McHenry, M. (2009). Policy options when giving negative externalities market value: Clean energy policymaking and restructuring the Western Australian energy sector. *Energy Policy*, *37*(4), 1423–1431.

Metcalf, G. E., & Weisbach, D. (2012). Linking policies when tastes differ: Global climate policy in a heterogeneous world. *Review of Environmental Economics and Policy*. *6*(1), 110–129.

Milliman, S. R., & Prince, R. (1989). Firm incentives to promote technological change in pollution control. *Journal of Environmental Economics and Management*, *17*(3), 247–265.

Mohnen, P., & Röller, L. H. (2005). Complementarities in innovation policy. *European Economic Review*, *49*(6), 1431–1450.

Montgomery, W. D. (1972). Markets in licenses and efficient pollution control programs. *Journal of Economic Theory*, *5*(3), 395–418.

Moreira, S., Vasconcelos, L., & Silva Santos, C. (2018). Occupational health indicators: Exploring the social and decent work dimensions of green jobs in Portugal. *Work*, *61*(2), 189–209.

Nagy, R. L., Hagspiel, V., & Kort, P. M. (2021). Green capacity investment under subsidy withdrawal risk. *Energy Economics*, *98*, 105259.

Nelson, R. R. (1959). The simple economics of basic scientific research. *Journal of Political Economy*, *67*(3), 297–306.

Nemet, G. F. (2006). Beyond the learning curve: Factors influencing cost reductions in photovoltaics. *Energy Policy*, *34*(17), 3218–3232.

Newell, R. G., & Siikamäki, J. (2014). Nudging energy efficiency behavior: The role of information labels. *Journal of the Association of Environmental and Resource Economists*, *1*(4), 555–598.

Nguyen, Q. K. (2025). Green finance, climate risk and financial stability: Evidence from ASEAN+ 4 countries. *Environmental and Sustainability Indicators*, *28*, 100922.

Noland, J. K., Hjelmeland, M. N., & Korpås, M. (2024). Will energy-hungry AI create a baseload power demand boom? *IEEE Access*, *12*, 110353–110360.

OECD. (2007). *Energy Security and Climate Policy-Assessing Interactions*.

OECD. (2008). *Taxation, innovation, and the environment – The Spanish case*. Available at www.olis.oecd.org/olis/2008doc.nsf/linkto/com-env-epoc-ctpa–cfa (assessed on 17.05.2020).

OECD. (2010). *Taxation, innovation and the environment. Executive summary.* https://www.oecd.org/env/tools-evaluation/46177075.pdf,dateaccessed:2018-10-22 (accessed 22.10.2018).

OECD. (2015) *OECD environmental performance reviews: Spain 2015* (p. 236). OECD Publishing.

OECD. (2020). Why does eco-innovation differ in service firms? Some insights from Spain. *Business Strategy and the Environment*, 29(3), 918–938.

OECD. (2025a). *Corporate income tax, investment, and the Net-Zero Transition, OECD Report written by L. Dressler and R. Warwick.*

OECD (2025b). *Packaging and sequencing policies for more effective climate action* (OECD Net Zero+ Policy Papers, No. 10). https://doi.org/10.1787/fced4e28-en

Ohlendorf, N., Jakob, M., Minx, J. C., Schröder, C., & Steckel, J. C. (2021). Distributional impacts of carbon pricing: A meta-analysis. *Environmental and Resource Economics*, *78*(1), 1–42.

Organisation for Economic Co-operation and Development. (2022). Best available techniques (BAT) for preventing and controlling industrial pollution—Activity 6: Cross-country analysis of selected sectors for comparison. https://www.oecd.org/content/dam/oecd/en/publications/reports/2022/09/best-available-techniques-bat-for-preventing-and-controlling-industrial-pollution-activity-6-cross-country-analysis-of-selected-sectors-for-comparison_d6931c46/068bce3f-en.pdf

Ortega, M., del Río, P., Ruiz, P., & Thiel, C. (2015). Employment effects of renewable electricity deployment. A novel methodology. *Energy*, *91*, 940–951.

Ostrom, E. (1990). *Governing the commons: The evolution of institutions for collective action.* Cambridge University Press.

Ostrom, E., Gardner, R., & Walker, J. (1994). *Rules, games, and common-pool resources.* University of Michigan Press.

Our World in Data. (2025). *Modern renewable energy consumption.* https://ourworldindata.org/grapher/modern-renewable-energy-consumption (accessed 2.12.2025).

Oussama, S., & Oluyede, N. (2022). Understanding the drivers of eco-innovation efficiency: A systematic overview. *Journal of Policy Options*, *5*(4), 15–21.

Ozusaglam, S., Kesidou, E., & Wong, C. Y. (2018). Performance effects of complementarity between environmental management systems and environmental technologies. *International Journal of Production Economics*, *197*, 112–122.

Pahle, M., Burtraw, D., Flachsland, C., Kelsey, N., Biber, E., Meckling, J., & Zysman, J. (2018). Sequencing to ratchet up climate policy stringency. *Nature Climate Change*, *8*(10), 861–867.

Pakizer, K., Lieberherr, E., Farrelly, M., Bach, P. M., Saurí, D., March, H., & Binz, C. (2023). Policy sequencing for early-stage transition dynamics–A process model and comparative case study in the water sector. *Environmental Innovation and Societal Transitions*, *48*, 100730.

Parrilli, M. D., Balavac-Orlić, M., & Radicic, D. (2023). Environmental innovation across SMEs in Europe. *Technovation*, *119*, 102541.

Peñasco, C., del Río, P., & Romero-Jordán, D. (2017). Analysing the role of international drivers for eco-innovators. *Journal of International Management*, *23*(1), 56–71.

Petersen, A., Reguant, M., & Segura, L. (2024). Measuring the impact of wind power and intermittency. *Energy Economics*, *129*, 107200.

Philibert, C. (2011). Interactions of policies for renewable energy and climate. *OECD Report.*

Pigou, A. C. (1920). *The economics of welfare*. McMillan.

Popp, D. (2002). Induced innovation and energy prices. *American Economic Review*, *92*(1), 160–180.

Popp, D. (2006). International innovation and diffusion of air pollution control technologies: The effects of NOX and SO 2 regulation in The US, Japan, and Germany. *Journal of Environmental Economics and Management*, *51*(1), 46–71.

Popp, D., Newell, R. G., & Jaffe, A. B. (2009). *Energy, the environment, and technological change* (NBER Working Paper No. 14832). National Bureau of Economic Research. https://doi.org/10.3386/w14832

Popp, D. (2019). Environmental policy and innovation: *A* decade of research (NBER working paper). National Bureau of Economic Research.

Porter, M. E. (1991). Towards a dynamic theory of strategy. *Strategic Management Journal*, *12*(S2), 95–117.

Porter, M. E., & van der Linde, C. (1995). Toward a new conception of the environment–competitiveness relationship. *Journal of Economic Perspectives*, *9*(4), 97–118.

Pujari, D. (2006). Eco-innovation and new product development: Understanding the influences on market performance. *Technovation*, *26*(1), 76–85.

Rave, T., Goetzke, F., & Larch, M. (2011). *The determinants of environmental innovations and patenting: Germany reconsidered* (Ifo working paper). Ifo Institute.

Reichenbach, J., & Requate, T. (2012). Subsidies for renewable energies in the presence of learning effects and market power. *Resource and Energy Economics*, *34*(2), 236–254.

Ren, S., He, D., Zhang, T., & Chen, X. (2019). Symbolic reactions or substantive pro-environmental behaviour? An empirical study of corporate environmental performance under the government's environmental subsidy scheme. *Business Strategy and the Environment*, *28*(6), 1148–1165.

Ren, X., Zhang, X., Yan, C., & Gozgor, G. (2022). Climate policy uncertainty and firm-level total factor productivity: Evidence from China. *Energy Economics*, *113*, 106209.

Rennings, K. (2000). Redefining innovation—eco-innovation research and the contribution from ecological economics. *Ecological Economics*, *32*(2), 319–332.

Rennings, K., Ziegler, A., & Zwick, T. (2004). The effect of environmental innovations on employment changes: An econometric analysis. *Business Strategy and the Environment*, *13*(6), 374–387.

Requate, T. (1995). Incentives to adopt new technologies under different pollution-control policies. *International Tax and Public Finance*, *2*(2), 295–317.

Requate, T. (2005). Timing and commitment of environmental policy, adoption of new technology, and repercussions on R&D. *Environmental and Resource Economics*, *31*(2), 175–199.

Resende, M., Strube, E., & Zeidan, R. (2014). Complementarity of innovation policies in Brazilian industry: An econometric study. *International Journal of Production Economics*, *158*, 9–17.

Rodrik, D. (2014). Green industrial policy. *Oxford Review of Economic Policy*, *30*(3), 469–491.

Rogge, K. S., & Reichardt, K. (2016). Policy mixes for sustainability transitions: An extended concept and framework for analysis. *Research Policy*, *45*(8), 1620–1635.

Romer, P. M. (1990). Endogenous technological change. *Journal of Political Economy*, *98*(5, Part 2), S71–S102.

Sendstad, L. H., Hagspiel, V., Mikkelsen, W. J., Ravndal, R., & Tveitstøl, M. (2022). The impact of subsidy retraction on European renewable energy investments. *Energy Policy*, *160*, 112675.

Shang, B. (2023). The poverty and distributional impacts of carbon pricing: Channels and policy implications. *Review of Environmental Economics and Policy*, *17*(1), 64–85.

Shi, H., & Zhou, Q. (2024). Government R&D subsidies, environmental regulation and corporate green innovation performance. *Finance Research Letters*, *69*, 106088.

Simon, H. A. (1955). A behavioral model of rational choice. *The Quarterly Journal of Economics*, *69*(1), 99–118.

Souto, J. E., & Rodriguez, A. (2015). The problems of environmentally involved firms: Innovation obstacles and essential issues in the achievement of environmental innovation. *Journal of Cleaner Production*, *101*, 49–58.

Stavins, R. N. (2003). Experience with market-based environmental policy instruments. In *Handbook of environmental economics* (Vol. 1, pp. 355–435). Elsevier.

Suzuki, E., & Pirlea, A. F. (2025). *World Population Day: Trends and demographic changes*. World Bank.

Tao, H., Zhuang, S., Xue, R., Cao, W., Tian, J., & Shan, Y. (2022). Environmental finance: An interdisciplinary review. *Technological Forecasting and Social Change*, *179*, 121639.

Metcalf, E., & Tchobanoglous, G. (2014). *Wastewater Engineering Treatment and Resource Recovery* (5th ed.). McGraw-Hill Education, https://repositori.mypolycc.edu.my/handle/123456789/4586, date accessed: 28.12.2025

Tchorzewska, K. B. (2020). Essays on Environmental Policy and Green Investment, Doctoral dissertation, University of Barcelona.

Tchorzewska, K. B. (2024). A lost opportunity? Environmental investment tax incentive and energy efficient technologies. *Environmental and Resource Economics*, *87*(12), 3301–3333.

Tchorzewska, K. B. (2025a) Summary of studies on the impacts of clean transition policies on employment in the European union and eu just transition policies: Draft. Report by the European Commission. https://unfccc.int/documents/649938 (accessed 03.12.2025).

Tchorzewska, K. B. (2025b). Environmental investment tax credit: The proportional effects. *Eurasian Business Review*, *15*, 1–25.

Tchorzewska, K. B., Del Rio, P., Garcia-Quevedo, J., & Martinez-Ros, E. (2025). Carrot first, stick second? Environmental policy-mix sequencing and green technologies. *Technological Forecasting and Social Change*, *210*, 123835.

Tchorzewska, K. B., Pathak, Y., & Jednorog, R. (2026a) *How climate change will affect the energy supply? Empirical evidence from Poland* (working paper).

Tchorzewska, K. B., Pathak, Y., & Jednorog, R. (2026b) *Electric shadows. Coal power plant failures and air quality dynamics* (working paper).

Tchórzewska, K. B., Garcia-Quevedo, J., & Martinez-Ros, E. (2022). The heterogeneous effects of environmental taxation on green technologies. *Research Policy*, *51*(7), 104541.

Thaler, R. H., & Sunstein, C. R. (2021). *Nudge: The final edition*. Penguin.

Tietenberg, T., & Lewis, L. (2023). *Environmental and natural resource economics*. Routledge.

Tinbergen, J. (1952). *On the theory of economic policy*. North-Holland Publishing Company.

Triguero, A., Moreno-Mondéjar, L., & Davia, M. A. (2013). Drivers of different types of eco632 innovation in European SMEs. *Ecological Economics*, *92*, 25–33.

Tuominen, M., Rajala, A., & Möller, K. (2004). How does adaptability drive firm innovativeness. *Journal of Business Research*, *57*(5), 495–506.

UNEP. (2025). *Eco-innovation*. https://www.unep.org/eco-innovation

United Nations Environment Programme. (2007, June 26). Environmental agreements and cleaner production. https://www.unep.org/resources/report/environmental-agreements-and-cleaner-production

Uyarra, E., Shapira, P., & Harding, A. (2016). Low carbon innovation and enterprise growth in the UK: Challenges of a place-blind policy mix. *Technological Forecasting and Social Change*, *103*, 264–272.

Van den Bergh, J. C. J. M., Castro, J., Drews, S., Exadaktylos, F., Foramitti, J., Klein, F., & Savin, I. (2021). Designing an effective climate-policy mix: Accounting for instrument synergy. *Climate Policy*, *21*(6), 745–764.

Varian, H. R. (2014). *Intermediate microeconomics with calculus: A modern approach*. WW Norton & Company.

Vasileiou, E., Georgantzis, N., Attanasi, G., & Llerena, P. (2024). The role of innovation portfolio in green innovation decisions: A study of French and Italian firms. *Technovation*, *130*, 102921.

Veugelers, R. (2012). Which policy instruments to induce clean innovating? *Research Policy*, *41*(10), 1770–1778.

Vivanco, M. G., Garrido, J. L., Martín, F., Theobald, M. R., Gil, V., Santiago, J. L., Lechon, Y., Gamarra, A. R., Sanchez, E., Alberto, A., & Bailador, A. (2021). Assessment of the effects of the Spanish national air pollution control programme on air quality. *Atmosphere*, *12*(2), 158.

Wallsten, S. J. (2000) The effects of government-industry R&D programs on private R&D: The case of the small business innovation research programme, *RAND Journal of Economics*, *31*(1), 82–100.

Wang, L., Ma, P., Song, Y., & Zhang, M. (2023). How does environmental tax affect enterprises' total factor productivity? Evidence from the reform of environmental fee-to-tax in China. *Journal of Cleaner Production*, *413*, 137441.

Wang, Y., Akhtar, R., Mu, W., Lv, W., & Li, L. (2025). Government subsidy and enterprise green innovation: Evidence from Chinese enterprises. *Polish Journal of Environmental Studies*, *34*(5), 1–179.

World Bank, International Energy Agency, International Renewable Energy Agency, United Nations Statistics Division, World Health Organisation. (2024). Tracking SDG 7: The Energy Progress Report 2024. https://www.irena.org/-/media/Files/IRENA/Agency/Publication/2024/Jun/IRENA_Tracking_SDG7_energy_progress_2024.pdf

World Energy Council (2024). *World Energy Trilemma 2024: Evolving with resilience and justice*. https://www.worldenergy.org/transition-toolkit/world-energy-trilemma-framework?utm_source=chatgpt.com (accessed 04.12.2025).

Wu, R. (2023). Environmental management, environmental innovation, and productivity growth: A global firm-level investigation. *Environment and Development Economics*, *28*(5), 449–468.

Wu, Z., Fan, X., Zhu, B., Xia, J., Zhang, L., & Wang, P. (2022). Do government subsidies improve innovation investment for new energy firms: A quasi-natural experiment of China's listed companies. *Technological Forecasting and Social Change*, *175*, 121418.

Xie, X., Zhu, Q., & Wang, R. (2019). Turning green subsidies into sustainability: How green process innovation improves firms' green image. *Business Strategy and the Environment*, *28*(7), 1416–1433.

Yamazaki, A. (2017). Jobs and climate policy: Evidence from British Columbia's revenue-neutral carbon tax. *Journal of Environmental Economics and Management*, *83*, 197–216.

Ying, Y., Wang, S., & Liu, Y. (2022). Make bricks without straw: Eco-innovation for resource constrained firms in emerging markets. *Technovation*, *114*, 102517.

Yip, C. M. (2018). On the labor market consequences of environmental taxes. *Journal of Environmental Economics and Management*, *89*, 136–152.

Zhang, D. (2022). Do heterogenous subsides work differently on environmental innovation? A mechanism exploration approach. *Energy Economics*, *114*, 106233.

Zhang, F., Yin, X., Zhang, H., & Zhan, X. (2024). Does environmental regulation enhance servitization in aspirant markets? Evidence from China's manufacturing sector. *Technovation*, *131*, 102952.

Zhao, L., Zhang, Y., Sadiq, M., Hieu, V. M., & Ngo, T. Q. (2023). Testing green fiscal policies for green investment, innovation and green productivity amid the COVID-19 era. *Economic Change and Restructuring*, *56*(5), 2943–2964.

Zhou, Q., Li, T., & Gong, L. (2022). The effect of tax incentives on energy intensity: Evidence from China's VAT reform. *Energy Economics*, *108*, 105887.

Zwick, E., & Mahon, J. (2017). Tax policy and heterogeneous investment behavior. *American Economic Review*, *107*(1), 217–248.

Index

Note: *Italic* and **bold** page numbers refer to figures and tables, respectively. Page numbers followed by 'n' refer to notes.